GCSE Drama

Live Theatre Evaluation

Annie Fox

Published in 2021 by Illuminate Publishing Limited, an imprint of Hodder Education, an Hachette UK Company, Carmelite House, 50 Victoria Embankment, London EC4Y 0DZ

Orders: Please visit www.illuminatepublishing.com
or email sales@illuminatepublishing.com

British Library Cataloguing-in-Publication Data

A catalogue record for this book is available from the British Library.

ISBN 978-1-912820-97-9

Produced by DZS Grafik, Printed in Bosnia & Herzegovina

04.22

The publishers' policy is to use papers that are natural, renewable and recyclable products made from wood grown in sustainable forests. The logging and manufacturing processes are expected to conform to the environmental regulations of the country of origin.

Every effort has been made to contact copyright holders of material produced in this book. Great care has been taken by the author and publishers to ensure that either formal permission has been granted for the use of copyright material reproduced, or that copyright material has been used under the provision of fair-dealing guidelines in the UK – specifically that it has been used sparingly, for the purpose of quotation, criticism or review, and has been properly acknowledged. If notified, the publisher will be pleased to rectify any errors or omissions at the earliest opportunity.

Editor: Roanne Charles, abc Editorial
Design and layout: emc design ltd
Cover design: Neil Sutton at Cambridge Design Consultants
Cover photograph of *The Jungle* (Playhouse Theatre): Marc Brenner

Grateful acknowledgement is given for use of the following extracts

p20: Extract from 'Lucian Msamati on Amadeus: "Colour-blind casting? I want you to see my colour"', Interview by Arifa Akbar, *The Guardian* 14.7.20, © Arifa Akbar / The Guardian.

p20: Extract from 'Present Laughter review – Andrew Scott dazzles in Coward's classic comedy' by Michael Billington, *The Guardian* 26.6.19, © Michael Billington / The Guardian.

p30: Extract from 'Design is a political act – let's use it to reshape the future' by Rosie Elnile, *The Stage* 20.8.20, © Rosie Elnile / The Stage.

p40: Extract from '"Hamilton" costume designer on how he streamlined 18th century looks for a 21st century show' by Patrick Pacheco, *LA Times* 11.6.16, © Patrick Pacheco / LA Times.

p40: Extract from 'Costume designer Nicky Gillibrand: "I set myself the challenge of finding vintage pieces I can adapt"', by Liz Hoggard, *The Stage* 2.12.19, © Liz Hoggard / The Stage.

p50: Extract from 'Prema Mehta: "The beauty and atmosphere of the Sam Wanamaker is unique"' Interview by Kate Wyver, *The Stage* 13.1.20, © Kate Wyver / The Stage.

p50: Extract from 'An Interview with Tim Deiling', © City Theatrical 2019.

p60: Extract from 'Sound Design is a Creative Discipline: An Interview with Pete Malkin' by leoemercer, *Oxford Culture Review* 6.19.16, © leoemercer / Oxford Culture Review.

p60: Extract from *One Man, Two Guvnors, National Theatre Learning Background pack*, Interview with Grant Olding by Adam Penford, © Adam Penford / Grant Olding / National Theatre.

CONTENTS

INTRODUCTION

How to use this book

This book offers guidance on how to approach the live theatre component or unit of your GCSE Drama course. This is the component in which you will write about a theatrical production you have seen.

The demands of each exam board vary in some ways, but they all expect you to respond to, analyse and evaluate a live performance, whether that was seen in a theatre or as a recorded or live-streamed production.

Depending on the exam board, you may have the choice to write about actors' performances or a specific design specialism; you may answer a single question or be guided to write about a combination of designs or performances. Whatever the specific question or questions, you must be prepared to show that you understand how live theatre works, its technical production elements and how the choices made by actors and designers create meaning and effects.

Features to help you get the most from the book

LIVE THEATRE EVALUATION

Extracts from sample answers

The following two extracts are from candidate-style responses that analyse and evaluate a costume design.

TIPS:

Advice for success in the exam and suggestions on how to avoid common errors.

 TIP

These extracts are based on particular candidates' experience of certain performances. They are only example points that could be made, not model answers. Even if you saw the same performance, your recollection, notes and reactions will be different.

TASK 5

1   Read the sample responses and put:
   ▶ **D** next to any performance details
   ▶ **T** next to any correct terminology.

2   Note any points which you believe are analysis (**A**) of the set and any which you would consider evaluation (**E**).
   One example of each has been done for you.

TASKS:

Practical activities to improve your learning.

Ⓐ

In *Amadeus*, the costume designer conveyed two periods, 18th-century Vienna and the present day. The latter was mainly represented by the two assistants and the musicians, dressed in contemporary black clothing. In contrast, the main characters wore elaborate period clothing. Ⓣ Salieri's costumes often suggested his wealth, using rich fabrics such as velvet, silk and satin, whose sheen caught the lights. First seen as an older man in a robe of dark purple and gold, with a quilted collar and cuffs, when he suddenly becomes young, a period wig is added. Other bewigged characters in period costumes enter, demonstrating that we are going back in Salieri's memory. His 'younger' costume consists of a frock coat in green, a waistcoat, a white lace collar and gold buttons, embroidery and embellishments. Ⓓ He wears white stockings and heeled shoes adorned

THEATRE IN PRACTICE:

Production photographs, articles and quotes from theatre makers which provide examples of, and insight into, live theatre.

Public Theater readings. To show the first audiences how the two eras would meet in the look of the show, Tazewell started with a simple parchment-toned silhouette of vest, breeches and boots that then gave way to the blue coats, red trim and brass buttons of Washington's Continental Army. Most important, no wigs.

The success of the workshop resulted in two guiding principles: First, period from the neck down and modern from the neck up; and second, strip away all the embroidered detail of the 18th century so the audience could move past the distraction of artifice to the story itself.'

TERMINOLOGY:

Vocabulary is highlighted to help you understand how drama works and to express your ideas fluently and appropriately. These terms are defined in the glossary at the back of the book as a reference resource.

🎭 **THEATRE IN PRACTICE**

Nicky Gillibrand, Costume Designer on *The Duchess of Malfi* at the Almeida Theatre (in *The Stage*):

The **Jacobean revenge tragedy** has been cut … and is in modern dress. 'The play feels very current,' Gillibrand says, 'so I'm trying to find pieces that indicate a historical quality. Everyone is in evening wear. Rebecca [Frecknell, the director] used the word "**couture**" and she wanted quite a limited palette, so we've ended up with tones of black and white, and then flesh tones, which in itself is quite challenging. I am trying to describe the Italian court with the choices I make, and push the design so it has a wealthy quality about it, from the Duchess and her brothers, trickling down to the rest of the court.'

PRACTICE QUESTIONS:

A range of exam-type questions to help you get used to the typical wording and style.

SAMPLE ANSWERS:

Candidate-style responses for you to evaluate and annotate, and to show you where marks might be lost or gained.

TASK 6

1 Choose a lighting design from a play you have seen and answer the following question:

> Analyse and evaluate two key moments from the lighting design in the production and explain how it creates mood and atmosphere for the audience.

TASK 3

1 Recall a play you have seen and any important ways in which the lighting was used to reinforce a theme or support meaning.
2 Write a paragraph explaining the effect of this use of lighting. For example:

> In this production, which shows the darker side of life in an American high school, the lighting designer used bright, clean, colourful LED washes for the more upbeat scenes. To further emphasise the school setting, LEDs, in what looked like old-fashioned fluorescent strip lights, were hung from the ceiling of the set. For the prom, moving gobos created a disco-ball effect. In the contrasting sections where the protagonist directly addressed the audience, a sharp-edged spotlight cast a harsh white circular pattern around him. When he was speaking, the rest of the stage was shadowy, with blue gels creating an ominous feeling. The combination of the bright high school lights with the darker direct address sections captures the two sides of high school life.

 Directions to online versions of grids and charts for you to download and use for more extended writing. These can be found at illuminatepublishing.com.

How is live theatre assessed?

The live theatre question is part of the written exam, but the style of questions varies between exam boards. You will always, however, need to identify clearly the production you have seen, including the date and venue. The play must be a different one from the set text you have studied in class.

Exam board	AQA	OCR	Edexcel	WJEC	Eduqas
Section	Section C: Live Theatre Production	Section B: Live Theatre Evaluation	Section B: Live Theatre Evaluation	Section B: Live Theatre Review	Section B: Live Theatre Review
Available marks	32	30	15	15	15
How many questions must I answer?	One, from a choice of three.	You will be asked one question.	You will be asked two questions.	One, from a choice of two.	One, from a choice of two.
Are notes allowed for this section of the exam?	No.	No.	Yes. You can bring in theatre evaluation notes of up to 500 words.	No.	No.

CHAPTER 1

COMPONENTS OF LIVE THEATRE

When you go to the theatre to watch a show, you will be influenced by many elements, including the script, the direction, the actors and the design. For your evaluation in the exam, you will be guided to write about performances or design, or a combination of these.

PRODUCTION ELEMENTS

The range of elements you might write about includes:

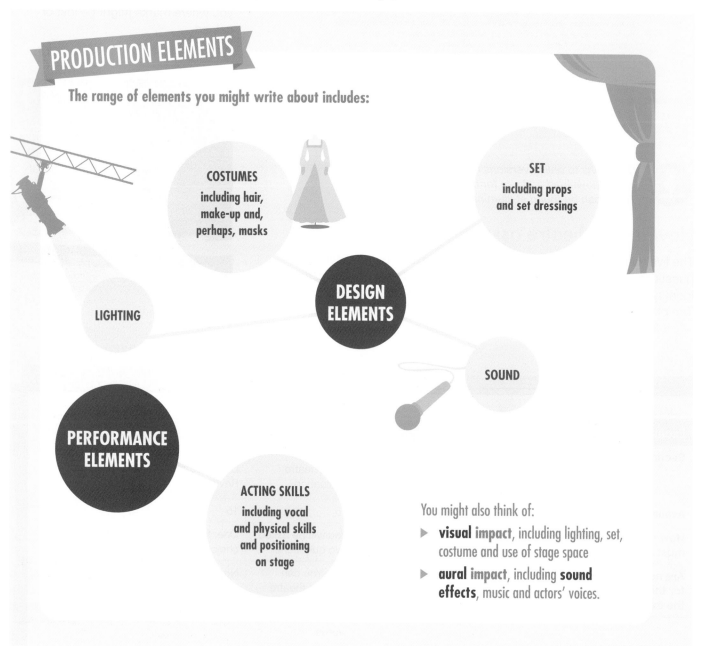

COSTUMES
including hair, make-up and, perhaps, masks

SET
including props and set dressings

LIGHTING

DESIGN ELEMENTS

SOUND

PERFORMANCE ELEMENTS

ACTING SKILLS
including vocal and physical skills and positioning on stage

You might also think of:

▶ **visual impact**, including lighting, set, costume and use of stage space

▶ **aural impact**, including **sound effects**, music and actors' voices.

Assessing the effect or impact on the audience

Part of the evaluative process is to consider how a production element affects the audience's experience of the play. You might observe, for example, that 'the lighting was dim with a grey tinge' and that the effect of this was to 'create a sense of danger and mystery for the audience.'

TIP

You will never be asked to summarise the plot of the play or write out the cast list. The focus is on your **understanding** and **analysis** of the design and performance elements.

TASK 1

Look at the following descriptions of production elements. Match each one to its likely effect or impact on the audience. An example has been done for you.

PRODUCTION ELEMENT

- The actors stood in clearly defined pools of blue light.
- The costumes used bright primary colours and had playful accessories in the shape of animals.
- Classical music blasted out from **speakers** arranged around the audience.
- The set was huge, with oversized, lumbering towers formed by tall grey **scaffolding**.
- The actors ran out into the audience and pulled people onto the stage.

EFFECT

- We felt excited and somewhat frightened by the interaction.
- The set made the characters seem small and helpless.
- The audience laughed at the comical outfits.
- This created a sombre mood and suggested that the characters were lost in their own worlds.
- We felt surrounded by the sound and overwhelmed by the **intensity** and **volume** of it.

TASK 2

Think of a production you have seen. Describe three detailed production elements and the effect of each of those elements.

TIP

Consider any responses you had yourself and observed in the audience. Did you and/or the rest of the audience laugh, jump with fright, gasp in surprise, grow restless, applaud or in any other way react to the production?

Genre, style and context

When evaluating a production, you may need to refer to its **genre**, **style** or **context**.

Genre

Genre is the category or type of play it is. The production you view may be one from a number of genres, such as a musical, like *Wicked*, a Greek tragedy, like *Antigone*, or a comedy, like *The Play That Goes Wrong*.

Theatrical genres have **conventions** associated with them, so part of your evaluation of the production elements might involve how well they support the expectations of that genre.

Style

The style of the production is the way in which the elements are done. Two major theatrical styles are **naturalistic** (realistic, believable, lifelike) and **stylised** (not realistic, heightened), but there are many other aspects of style. The main style for a comedy like *The Play That Goes Wrong*, for example, might be **physical comedy** or **farce**. Its other stylistic choices might include **audience interaction**, breaking the **fourth wall** and **synchronised** movement. You will need to evaluate the success of choices like these.

Context

The context of a play is the **period** and location in which it is set, as well as the historical, social and cultural factors which influence it.

TIP

Words highlighted in blue, throughout the book, are defined in the glossary at the back of the book.

Artistic intentions

Most plays are put on with a purpose, and the director will have a vision, **artistic intention** or **concept** of what they hope to achieve. A company might choose to produce a play in order to explore a particular theme, such as civil rights, the evils of war or the difficulties of family life. Even the most outrageous comedy or light-hearted musical will probably have a message, for example about the importance of perseverance, the value of friendship or the power of overcoming obstacles.

As you watch a play, consider how the different production elements support the play's meaning and artistic intentions, and how successful they are.

TASK 3

Think of a production you have seen and identify its:

▶ genre

▶ style

▶ context

▶ artistic intentions, concept and themes.

▲ *Lorraine Hansberry's* A Raisin in the Sun *explores civil rights in 1950s America.*

TASK 4

Imagine you been asked to design a production of Shakespeare's *Macbeth* which highlights the Macbeths' thirst for power. Make a bullet-point list of how the lighting, costumes, set and sound could all reinforce this artistic intention. For example, you might update the production to a particular political period, or your design could show the wealth and power of the king, or you might use colours (such as gold), symbols or abstract images to highlight this theme.

CHAPTER 2

PREPARING TO VIEW A THEATRE PERFORMANCE

TIP

Even if you are seeing a recorded production, you should be aware of when, where and on what type of stage it happened.

TIP

Most exam boards do not allow notes in the exam, so use the grids in this book to help you identify and recall production details **before** the exam.

Two skills which will help you to write about live theatre are research and note-taking.

Research

You might see your live theatre production already armed with an understanding of the play. This could involve:

▶ reading all or some of the play

▶ reading reviews of the production

▶ researching the time or location in which the play is set

▶ finding out about the cast and creative team, including the actors and designers.

On the other hand, you might see the show without any advance information, and research more about it afterwards.

Whatever your approach, you can use the grid below to check your understanding of the production.

Research notes	
Name of production	
Date of performance	
Name of theatre, or performance space	
Synopsis	
When and where is the play set?	
Main characters and the actors playing them	
Director and designers	
New play or revival of an older play?	
Why do you think it is being staged?	
Key themes	
Critical reaction to the production: ▶ Notable reviews　　▶ Has it won awards? ▶ Any aspect of the production　▶ Was there anything controversial 　particularly admired or criticised　about the production?	
Any key features that have been remarked on that you were particularly looking forward to seeing?	
Your expectations of the performance: ▶ Traditional?　　▶ Funny? ▶ Exciting?　　▶ Frightening? ▶ Unusual?　　▶ Spectacular? ▶ Entertaining?	

Use the downloadable version from illuminatepublishing.com for fuller writing.

Note-taking

Whether you are going to see a production in a theatre or watching it remotely, you will need to develop your note-taking skills. The best notes convey important points quickly. You could create:

▶ bullet-point lists

▶ mind maps

▶ sketches

▶ grids from pre-made templates.

To avoid distracting others in the audience or missing important parts of the performance yourself, make your notes in the interval or soon after seeing the show, rather than during it. If you are watching a recording, you might have the advantage of watching it multiple times.

You will not be able to (nor should you) write about absolutely everything that occurs. Instead, notice significant moments, such as a sudden change in colour or the use of a **spotlight** which affects the mood.

Use the grid below to organise your notes and ensure that you cover a range of production elements.

 TIP

When taking notes quickly, don't write full sentences. Instead of, for example, 'On his first entrance, he is dressed in blue and grey satin', you could note, '1st entrance: blue/grey satin.'

 TIP

Use the glossary to learn about or remind yourself of the terminology in the grid below.

 TIP

Detailed charts for each production element are given in the following chapters.

Overview of live theatre note-taking			Notes	Impact/effect on you/audience
Production *Is it a famous play or a new one?*	▶ Title of play ▶ Where it was staged ▶ Staging configuration			
Performance *What was the first impression of a character?* *How effective were moments of conflict or emotion or the climax of the play?*	▶ Key moments (eg, entrances, turning points, climax) ▶ Skills: • Voice • Facial expressions • Gestures • Movement	• Characterisation • Use of stage space • Relationships with others		
Set Add a sketch.	▶ Size and shape ▶ Colours and textures ▶ Use of levels ▶ Furnishings	▶ Curtains/backdrops/flats ▶ Projections/**multimedia** ▶ Set changes/transitions		
Costumes	▶ Colours ▶ Fabrics ▶ Shape and fit ▶ Period	▶ Changes ▶ Accessories ▶ Make-up		
Lighting	▶ Colours ▶ Angles/positioning ▶ Special effects ▶ Transitions (blackouts, fades, and so on)			
Sound	▶ Types of sound ▶ Use of music ▶ Volume/amplification/direction	▶ Live or recorded ▶ Use of mics ▶ Position of speakers ▶ Special sound effects		
Concept / artistic intentions / meaning / message	▶ What did the theatre makers hope to achieve? ▶ How successful were they?			

 Put more complete responses into the version downloadable from illuminatepublishing.com.

CHAPTER 3

ANALYSING AND EVALUATING ACTING

▲ *Kristin Scott Thomas and Chiwetel Ejiofor in* The Seagull.

Acting is one of the most notable aspects of any theatrical production. Whether you are seeing an intimate one-person show, a large-scale musical or an **immersive**, **promenade** performance, you will undoubtedly be influenced by the quality of the performances.

Performance types and styles

Some styles of performance, might be:

- naturalistic
- stylised
- **contemporary**
- period
- comic
- dramatic
- a combination of some of the above.

The genre and style of the production will influence the type of acting you see. Here are some key features of each type.

Naturalistic acting

This is intended to create believable characters behaving in a realistic fashion. Some features of naturalistic acting include:

- small, meaningful **gestures**
- believable reactions
- accurate recreations of situations and conversations
- non-**stereotypical** characters.

Naturalistic acting usually involves ignoring the presence of the audience and observing the fourth wall between the audience and the stage. It is found in many different plays, from the 19th-century works of Ibsen and Chekhov to contemporary drama.

Stylised acting

This type of acting may involve heightened or exaggerated performances. It can be found in pantomimes, as well as a range of other theatre including some musicals, period drama and contemporary movement pieces. It may involve:

- synchronised movement
- dance
- stereotypical or larger-than-life characters
- speaking directly to the audience.

Contemporary acting

This acting is often used to convey modern stories and themes, for example, plays dealing with social or political concerns, or contemporary autobiographical plays. The acting will reflect modern uses of voice and movement and can range from naturalism to **storytelling**. Arinzé Kene's play *Misty*, for example, requires a variety of contemporary acting skills, as it blends rap, spoken word and stand-up comedy.

▲ *Cassio gets drunk in* Othello.

Period acting

These performances will reflect a certain period. Actors in a **Restoration comedy**, for example, may follow the acting styles of the 17th century, using handkerchiefs and fans for effects and carrying themselves with the typical **posture** of the era. Actors in a Shakespeare play may use appropriate vocal techniques when speaking the 16th-century verse. Actors in a **melodrama** or broad farce will use gestures and movements appropriate for the stereotypical period characters they are playing.

Actors in period plays may be skilful in moving in the costumes from that period and handling the props correctly.

Comic acting

Comedy involves skills such as precise timing and exaggerated facial expressions in order to make an audience laugh. Comic actors are often gifted in vocal skills such as **intonation** and **mimicry** and physical skills such as **pratfalls** and **double-takes**.

Dramatic acting

Here, actors use skills such as emotional range and compelling **characterisation** in order to interest and involve the audience in the situation of the characters.

Combination

Many performances will use several styles of acting. The original production of *Things I Know to Be True*, for example, combined naturalistic, believable conflict between the family members with stylised movement sequences. *A Taste of Honey* typically combines naturalistic scenes with stylised interludes inspired by the **music hall** tradition. A modern production of a Shakespeare play might combine the period demands of verse-speaking with more contemporary, spontaneous-seeming interactions. *Blood Brothers* often combines the naturalistic acting of the main characters with more stylised performances from the ensemble. It also contrasts the comedy of the early scenes with the emotional high drama of the ending.

TASK 1

1 Look at the production photographs on these pages and decide what type or types of acting are shown.

2 Choose one of the actors and describe them as much detail as you can. Consider, as appropriate:
   ▶ facial expressions
   ▶ gestures
   ▶ posture
   ▶ position on stage
   ▶ interaction with others
   ▶ any other distinctive features.

3 Look online for other production photographs and choose two to analyse for the performance styles.

▲ *Tim McInnerny, Alison Steadman and Janine Duvitski in* The Provok'd Wife.

Drama terminology: acting

In order to write accurately about acting, you need to understand the correct terminology.
Below are some useful words to help you describe and analyse what you have seen.

FACIAL EXPRESSION

Appearance of emotions, thoughts or feelings (or lack of them) through facial muscle movement or position of features, such as raised eyebrows, smile, scowl, narrowed eyes, pursed lips, gaping mouth.

TIMING/PACE

How quickly or slowly something is said or done, including the use of pause.

EYE CONTACT

Looking directly at someone who is looking back.

VOCAL SKILLS

Techniques involving the voice, including pitch, accent, diction, volume, emphasis and tone.

Also includes: vocal projection, such as breath control and diction, to make the voice carry.

POSTURE

How a character stands, such as upright, hunched or slumped.

CHARACTERISATION

The creation of a role through the performer's understanding and portrayal of the character's background, **motivations** and importance in the play.

DELIVERY OF LINES

How lines are said to convey their meaning. This could involve both vocal and physical skills.

EMOTIONAL RANGE

The ability to show a character's changing feelings.

USE OF STAGE SPACE

How much or little of the stage is used by the actor or actors; **blocking**, including use of levels and **proximity**.

INTERACTION WITH OTHERS

The relationships the actors build with each other; rapport between the performers; the proximity and movements between characters.

GESTURES

Movements of parts of the body, often hand, arms or head, such as waving, nodding or reaching out.

MOVEMENT

How the actor physically inhabits the character and travels around the stage. In some cases, this can be stylised, such as dance, lifts, or synchronised movement.

GAIT

How the character walks: limps, stomps, shuffles, strides, plods.

STANCE

The way the character stands, such as with feet wide apart or turned in.

TASK 2

Write a description of a performance you have seen using at least five of the terms given here.

 A downloadable version is available at illuminatepublishing.com.

TIP

If you can, find photographs of the production to remind yourself of key elements of the performances.

Making acting notes on the production you have seen

Use the chart below to make notes on the performance you saw. The prompts are suggestions to aid you, but won't cover every feature.

Ideally, make your notes as soon as you can after seeing the play.

Don't try to write about every moment: choose key performance points such as entrances, a conflict or turning point and the play's **climax** and ending.

Acting notes	
Production	
Main actor/s and character/s	
First impressions: ▶ posture ▶ gait ▶ gestures ▶ voice ▶ characterisation ▶ background/context	
Moments of conflict: ▶ use of voice ▶ emotional range ▶ movement ▶ proximity	
Turning points: changes in: ▶ volume ▶ posture ▶ facial expression	
Delivery of lines (two or three examples): Consider: ▶ emphasis ▶ tone ▶ pace ▶ pitch	
▶ Final impressions of the character. ▶ How does the audience feel about them?	

You may wish to print out more than one of these sheets to analyse different characters.

How is the acting shaped throughout the play?

As you watch the play, consider different ways in which the performances contribute to the characterisation, mood and meaning of the play. For example:

> Are there moments where the actor contributes to the comedy or drama?

> Does an actor show that their character changes or develops over the course of the play?

> Do the actor's movements surprise, shock or amuse the audience?

> Is the actor believable in the situations in the play?

> Does the actor react/respond to situations and other actors in a way that is engaging, believable and artistically satisfying?

> Are the actor's movements and speech clear enough to help the audience understand the play?

> Does the performance fit your understanding of the character?

Special challenges for actors

Some roles require special skills. These might include:

▶ ageing, either by playing a character older than themselves or showing a character at different ages in the play

▶ **multi-roling**, by playing more than one character

▶ singing and dancing

▶ mime

▶ stage fighting

▶ audience interaction.

In Peter Schaffer's play *Amadeus*, the actor portraying Salieri plays him as both a young man and an elderly dying man. In Enda Walsh's play *Misterman*, the actor playing Thomas portrays a disturbed, isolated young man as well as the various inhabitants of his village. Multi-roling is also an essential aspect of *The Woman in Black* and *The 39 Steps*, where actors play many different roles. The success with which the actors accomplish these tasks will be significant to how the audience receives their performances.

TASK 3

1 Think of a play you have seen and note any particular challenges for the actors.

2 Then choose a moment or two to describe in a few sentences. Discuss the effect on the audience of the acting in those scenes.

TASK 4

Use this mind map to begin selecting and exploring key moments in the play you have seen.

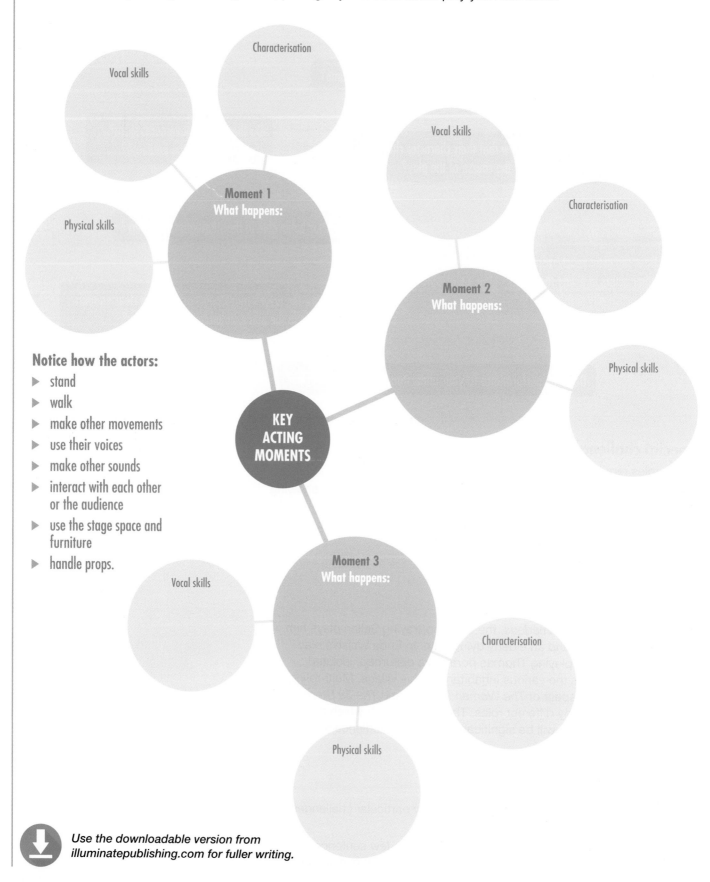

Vocal skills

Characterisation

Physical skills

Moment 1
What happens:

Vocal skills

Characterisation

Moment 2
What happens:

Physical skills

KEY ACTING MOMENTS

Notice how the actors:

▶ stand
▶ walk
▶ make other movements
▶ use their voices
▶ make other sounds
▶ interact with each other or the audience
▶ use the stage space and furniture
▶ handle props.

Vocal skills

Moment 3
What happens:

Characterisation

Physical skills

Use the downloadable version from illuminatepublishing.com for fuller writing.

TASK 5

Read the example response below, then highlight the drama terminology that the writer has used. Think about why the words you have highlighted are helpful.

Jenny Walser as the young Eva in Kindertransport.

In this production of *Kindertransport*, the actor playing Eva needs to age from a young girl of about nine to a teenager. The actor portrayed this change in her posture and **stance**. As a young girl, she stood upright, arms dangling at her side and feet slightly apart. When she didn't understand something, she would tilt her head to one side questioningly. She had a strong German accent and pronounced her English words carefully. When she arrived in England, she shouted, 'Stuff your stupid Hitler' with unabashed joy and jumped to her feet, banging on the (imaginary) windows of the train. These performance choices created audience sympathy for Eva.

In later scenes, as a teenager, after living in England for years, her German accent was almost entirely gone and her manner far more reserved. She hunched her shoulders and avoided making eye contact with her mother.

The actor believably accomplished this **transition** from open, innocent child to more complicated teenager, who has adopted a new identity. However, after following Eva's journey, I was disappointed to find so little of the appealing little girl apparent in the later scenes with her mother.

> 💡 **TIP**
>
> In the final paragraph of this response, where the candidate writes 'believably' (a positive comment) and 'disappointed' (a negative one), they have provided their personal response as an audience member, which will gain evaluation marks.

Using moments of change

Moments of change are useful for your analysis. In the example for *Kindertransport*, above, the writer has analysed the changes the actor made to show the character ageing. This might also be a focus in a review of *Blood Brothers*, for example, in which the main characters are shown at three different ages.

Besides physical changes, you might also look for emotional changes (such as when Romeo and Juliet fall in love), changes in status (as when Macbeth becomes king) or when a character disguises their identity (such as Viola dressing as a boy in *Twelfth Night*).

TASK 6

Recall a performance you have seen and note any moments when a character underwent a change in:

▶ age   ▶ emotions

▶ status   ▶ identity.

Then write a paragraph explaining how the actor used their acting skills to achieve this change.

THEATRE IN PRACTICE

The acclaimed actor Lucian Msamati (in *The Guardian*) on playing Iago in *Othello*:

'The challenge in all of it is to find the weakest point in any character which, I believe, is how you tap into the humanity of that character without judgement. Tapping into jealousy in itself is very easy. It's more difficult to tap into love for the victim of that jealousy; just as Salieri [in *Amadeus*] loves music, Iago loves Othello. I don't think you can commit yourself to such a dogged path of revenge or retribution unless you feel a great love – from great love comes great hurt and hate.'

▲ *Lucian Msamati (right) as Iago, with Hugh Quarshie as Othello.*

 TIP

Many actors strive to create well-rounded characters with virtues and faults or, as Msamati describes above, a combination of love and hate. When analysing a performance, consider whether the character is a complex one or a more simple, stereotypical hero or villain.

 THEATRE IN PRACTICE

In a *Guardian* review, the critic Michael Billington describes some of the skills of the actor Andrew Scott, who plays an egotistical star in the Noel Coward comedy *Present Laughter*:

'The chief joy, however, lies in watching Scott's display of Garry's boyish vanity. Accused of overacting, he beats himself about the face as if confirming the charge. Whenever mention is made of the Peer Gynt he was prevented from playing, Scott looks like a woebegone child deprived of a longed-for present. Funniest of all is his encounter with the playwright from Uckfield, Roland Maule, whom Luke Thallon invests with a lunging intensity. Prising his hand from Maule's ferocious grasp, Scott dips it in a beaker of cooling water. But, while capturing Garry's need to escape the clamorous demands of outsiders, Scott also has the orphaned look of stardom.'

TASK 7

Identify examples of Scott's acting skills in the Michael Billington review. Note words which indicate whether or not he thought the performance was successful.

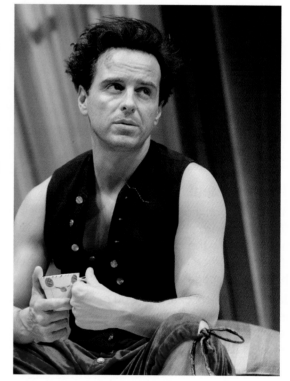

▲ *Andrew Scott as Garry Essendine in* Present Laughter.

 TIP

Many theatres, including the National Theatre and the Royal Shakespeare Company, have education departments. Find out if the theatre which produced the play you saw provides education packs. These can give helpful insights into the creative processes.

Performance evaluation

Beyond describing and analysing the performance you must evaluate it, considering whether or not it was effective and successful. This means doing more than just writing that it was 'good' or 'bad' or 'funny' or 'sad.' Think about the following:

Did the performance fulfil its purpose?
For example, if an actor was meant to represent a person of particular circumstances (age, nationality, background), were they successful?

Was the performance technically accomplished?
Did the actor meet the physical and vocal demands of the part?

Did the performance engage and interest the audience?
For example, were there moments that were surprising or moving or exciting?

Did the performance contribute to the mood and atmosphere?
For example, if the role was meant to be comic or frightening, did the performance achieve that?

Did the performance help you to understand the characters?
For example, if the characters were meant to be wealthy or careless, did the actors represent that?

Did the performance support the themes of the play?
For example, if the play was about poverty or injustice, did the performance convey that?

Sample analysis and evaluation

The two extracts below are from candidate-style responses that analyse and evaluate actors' performances.

TIP

These extracts are based on particular candidates' experience of certain performances. They are only example points that could be made, not model answers. Even if you saw the same performance, your recollection, notes and reactions will be different.

TASK 8

1 Read the sample responses and put:
   ▸ **D** next to any performance details
   ▸ **T** next to any correct terminology.

2 Note any points which you believe are analysis (**A**) of the performance and any which you would consider evaluation (**E**).

   One example of each has been done for you.

A

Adam Gillen, as Mozart in *Amadeus*, provides a contrasting performance to that of Lucian Msamati, who plays the plotting Salieri. Initially, the differences between the characters are shown by their gestures and vocal skills. When they are introduced to each other, Salieri lowers himself in a courtly bow, while Gillen's Mozart simply gives a playful little wave. **D** Msamati's voice is well-modulated and controlled, whereas Gillen's words often burst out, fast-paced and unpredictable, with a more youthful, informal dialect. **T** This provides an early indication of Salieri's ability to abide by the rules of Vienna's society, whereas Mozart's genius is uncontrolled. **A**

In his interpretation, Gillen seems to be influenced by modern figures such as punk musicians or stand-up comedians. I was uncertain about this choice at first, as it seemed so surprising for the era, but I came to see how it suited this partially modern take on the period. **E** Gillen stands with his toes pointed inwards, pulls comic faces and suddenly laughs. In the scene where he plays Salieri's tune by memory, instantly creating variations on it, he demonstrates both Mozart's love of music and his ease with it. While he plays, he sways and leans into the keyboard. Eventually he stands, rock-and-roll style, on the piano stool. At the end, he holds his arms out wide in a gesture asking for recognition. This contrasts well with Salieri's upright stance and tight, terse, 'No,' when asked if he wants to 'try a variation.'

Msamati's performance is nuanced and particularly touching in the scene where he listens to Mozart's music. At first, he sits, with his eyes closed, taking it in. He seems controlled by the music, suddenly standing when he hears a high oboe note. As he describes his physical reactions, he observes that he is 'trembling', which is echoed in his movements. He ably conveys the joy and agony of discovering a **composer** whose genius outdoes his own skills. He groans at the beauty of the music and shouts 'What is this?' in disbelief at the unlikeliness of someone as coarse as Mozart producing something so sublime. As his agitation grows, so does the pace of the speech.

Through their different performances the actors have perfectly set out the conflict at the centre of the play.

▲ *Adam Gillen and Lucian Msamati in* Amadeus.

B

Two performances which I found particularly compelling in *Approaching Empty* were Rina Fatania as Sameena and Kammy Darweish as Mansha. The two actors conveyed two different aspects of the immigrant experience, partly due to their being from different generations. Mansha's middle-aged character spends most of the play sitting in his office chair, occasionally occupying himself with minicab business tasks or turning to watch the TV. His hand gestures are often gentle or even pleading. By nature, he avoids fights, so his open hands and calming voice are suited to this.

It is very different from Sameena, whose first entrance makes a strong impression on the audience. She bursts in from stage left and angrily stomps on stage wanting to attack Mansha, who she feels has treated her disrespectfully. She juts her chin out and has one hand curled into a fist. Her speech is fast-paced as she spits out her complaints. Her rage is so unremitting and unexpected that it provokes appreciative laughter from the audience. It is only when Raf moves between her and Mansha and he concedes that she will get the next job that she backs off. From Fatania's performance, which was one of my favourites in the play, it is clear that Sameena has not had an easy life and has to fight for everything she gets.

Despite his relatively meek exterior, through the middle section of the play, Mansha begins to find some backbone, and this is conveyed through Darweish's performance. In the beginning of his conflict with Raf, he rubs his thumb and fingers together to indicate money, complaining, 'You've got the cream of it as well.' At another point, his gestures show the further deterioration of their relationship. When he finally decides to buy the business, he slowly stands and says in a solemn, low-pitched voice, 'Sell it to me.' This is a turning point, when Mansha decides he can make something more of his life. However, when they lose everything, Darweish's performance conveys this disappointment. His facial expression collapses into one of despair. His mouth is tight and he looks down. His hands are loose at his side. He appears to be fighting off tears when his son-in-law tells him off for being a loser. At the end of the play, he is a defeated man, and we feel sympathy for him. His performance made clear to me how difficult it is to get ahead in a world which seems to be set against him.

TIP

Part of the evaluation can be your particular reactions to a performance. These may be individual to you, but should be based on your experience as a thoughtful, well-informed audience member.

TASK 9

1   Choose a performance from a play you have seen and answer the following question:

> Analyse and evaluate one performance in the production and explain how it creates interest and meaning for the audience.

2   Then annotate your answer in the same way as the answers above for detail, terminology, analysis and evaluation.

TASK 10

Choose one of the questions below and make a detailed plan for how you would answer it:

> **a**   Analyse and evaluate how one actor's characterisation was used to support the themes of the production.
>
> **b**   Evaluate how one or more actors' skills conveyed the style and genre of the production in two scenes and the impact their choices had on you as an audience member.

TIP

You can use the acronym DATE to check your work:

Details

Analysis

Terminology

Evaluation.

▶ Advice on how to make plans can be found on pages 66–67 in this book.

CHAPTER 4

ANALYSING AND EVALUATING SET DESIGN

Set design is a very important element of theatrical production. The set is what you see on stage, from the **flies** to the floor. It can include many elements, including stage **furnishings**, **projections** and some **special effects**.

Styles of set

When you first observe the set, you should consider what type of set it is. It might be, for example:

naturalistic

fantasy

minimalist

stylised   a combination

The genre and style of the production will dictate the type of set employed. Here are some key features of each type.

Naturalistic set

These sets aim to accurately represent a period and location. They will have realistic details and, in some cases, may recreate a complete room with three walls, windows, doors, furnishings, and so on. Some designers will choose a selection of realistic objects, such as furniture and doors, but omit others. Designers of naturalistic sets often work at establishing the precise period of the play. A play that takes place in a rural community in the late 17th century, for example, would differ from one in a 1920s bar or a 21st-century office. For a historic drama, set designers will recreate the appearance of that period through their choice of materials and depiction of the architecture and furnishings. A contemporary naturalistic design might replicate locations and objects from the present day.

Minimalist set

This will be a very bare set, with only a few items, if any, on it. For example, there may be a few chairs, benches, **platforms** or boxes, often used in a variety of ways:

▶ Derek Jacobi's 2010 *King Lear* at the Donmar Warehouse was performed in what was essentially a cube of white boards.

▶ The RSC's 1978 *Macbeth* took place in a black-edged circle with some orange crates.

▶ Daniel Kitson's 2010 one-man show, *It's Always Right Now, Until It's Later,* used a bare stage except for a wooden chair and a series of suspended lightbulbs.

Sets like these are frequently seen in **episodic** productions where many different locations have to be suggested quickly, or when the focus is entirely on the actors and storytelling rather than any **spectacle**.

▲ *The 1997 production of* Waiting for Godot *at the Old Vic.*

Stylised set

These sets often have exaggerated or non-naturalistic features. A set might emphasise certain ideas or themes of the play. For example, the National Theatre set for *The Curious Incident of the Dog in the Night-Time* suggests the workings of Christopher's brain. It takes inspiration from laboratories, an incident board and a mathematical grid while offering the flexibility to represent many different locations. Meanwhile, a play about greed might have a set that is spray-painted gold. One about lack of privacy, might have surveillance cameras projecting the actors' movements onto a screen.

Fantasy set

This will create an unreal, perhaps supernatural world, such as a fairy tale or other imaginary place. A set for a pantomime, for example, might use bright colours and over-sized furnishings. There might be special effects, such as platforms which can be raised or lowered, or large set pieces like a carriage which can be wheeled onto the stage. Dramatic and glamorous effects might be created through draping, sparkling materials and lowering items from the flies.

▲ Wonder.land

Combination

Some designs will incorporate elements of two or more types of set design. The 2014 production of *Our Town* at the Almeida Theatre, for example, combined a minimalistic modern set of just a table and chairs for most of the play with a **reveal** at the end of a highly realistic period kitchen. For *The Nether*, the designer Es Devlin used several types of set design. There was a scene with minimalist tables and chairs, a stylised version of an internet world and then what could be considered a **fantasy** version of that world.

TASK 1

1 Look at the photographs on these pages and decide what type or types of set are shown.

2 Choose one of the sets and describe it in as much detail as you can. Consider:
  ▶ colours and materials used
  ▶ the positioning of the set and stage furnishings (upstage, downstage, and so on)
  ▶ the scale (size) of the set
  ▶ use of levels, doors, **ramps**, **stairs**, and so on
  ▶ any other distinctive features.

▲ June Moon

rama terminology: set

order to write accurately about set design, you need to understand the correct terminology.
low are some useful words to help you describe and analyse what you have seen.

LIES

The space above the stage, usually out of view of the audience, used to store or to ower ('fly') items onto the stage.

FLAT

A piece of scenery, often painted, mounted on a tall frame.

PROJECTION

A film or still image projected to form a theatrical backdrop.

FLY SYSTEM

A means of raising and lowering scenery or other items onto the stage using a system of ropes and pulleys. To lower scenery from this area is to 'fly a set in'.

WINGS / WING SPACE

n area to the side of the tage from which actors can nter and from which props, urnishings or scenery can be moved onto the stage.

BACKDROP

A large painted cloth hung, usually at the back of the stage, as part of the scenery.

CRIMS OR GAUZE

Curtains that might hang oose or be mounted on a rame, which, if lit a certain vay, are transparent.

PLATFORM

A raised area on the stage.

BOX SET

A setting of a complete room, often naturalistic, with three walls and a 'missing' fourth wall facing the audience.

TRAPDOOR

A door in the floor or ceiling of a stage allowing objects or performers to be dropped, lifted or lowered.

SCAFFOLDING

A large structure, usually of boards and metal poles, which creates different levels on a set.

SET DRESSINGS

Items on the set not used as props, but which create detail and interest, such as vases or framed paintings.

PROPS

Moveable items on the stage, including hand props that the actors can carry, including books, cups and phones.

DRAPES

Curtains or other hanging fabric.

CYCLORAMA

A large semi-circular stretched curtain or screen, usually positioned upstage. It often depicts a background, such as the sky.

FURNISHINGS

Furniture on the set, such as chairs, cushions and tables.

STAIRS

Steps from one level of the set to another. In some productions grand staircases are a design feature.

RAMPS

Sloped pathways which may be used for walking on or for wheeled transportation.

TRUCK

A platform on wheels upon which scenery can be mounted and moved.

REVOLVE

A large turntable device that can be turned to reveal a different setting.

FLOOR COVERINGS

Any covering of the stage floor, such as a wooden effect to appear like floorboards, or linoleum for a kitchen floor.

APRON

An area at the front of proscenium stages which is still visible to the audience when the curtains are closed.

TASK 2

Write a description of a set you have seen using at least five of the terms given here.

TASK 3

Draw a sketch of one important prop or piece of stage furnishing from a production you have seen and label it with notes on its use, colour, materials, size, and so on.

 A downloadable version is available at illuminatepublishing.com.

TIP

If you can, find photographs of the production to remind yourself of key elements of the set.

Making set design notes on the production you have seen

Use the chart below to make notes on the set in the show you saw. The prompts are suggestions to aid you, but won't cover every feature.

Ideally, make your notes as soon as you can after seeing the play.

Set design notes		Draw a basic sketch.
Production		
Type of set	▶ Naturalistic? ▶ Minimalist? ▶ Stylised? ▶ Fantasy? ▶ Period? ▶ Contemporary?	
Size, scale and positioning	▶ How big is the stage space and the scenery? ▶ Where key items are placed on the stage? ▶ Where are entrances and exits?	
Colours and materials	▶ What are the main colours used? ▶ Are the walls and fabrics plain or patterned? ▶ What is used in the set construction: fabrics, wood, plastic, metal and so on?	
Background	▶ Drapes or curtains? ▶ Flats? ▶ Backdrops? ▶ Cyclorama? ▶ Bare wall?	
Levels	▶ Platforms? ▶ Scaffolding? ▶ Ramps? ▶ Stairs?	
Technology	▶ Projections? ▶ Multimedia?	

How is the set used?

As you watch the play, consider different ways in which the set contributes to the mood and action of the play. For example:

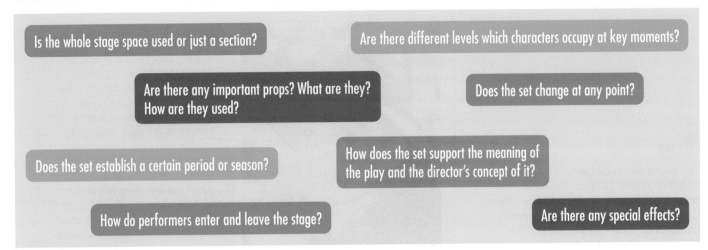

Is the whole stage space used or just a section?

Are there different levels which characters occupy at key moments?

Are there any important props? What are they? How are they used?

Does the set change at any point?

Does the set establish a certain period or season?

How does the set support the meaning of the play and the director's concept of it?

How do performers enter and leave the stage?

Are there any special effects?

Set design effects

Even in Shakespeare's time, there were some special stage effects, such as **trapdoors** in the floor and a space above the stage from which items or people could be lowered. In contemporary theatre, special effects may include:

▶ **revolves**

▶ moveable platforms

▶ falling snow, rain or petals

▶ items of set lowered from the flies

▶ scenic **gauze** which, when lit a certain way, reveals a scene behind it.

In Es Devlin's design for *Faith Healer* at the Donmar Warehouse in 2016, the set had the special effect of a rain curtain which appeared between scenes. It hid the set changes and evoked the other-worldly, rain-soaked, rural landscapes which the characters visit.

TASK 4

1 Recall a play you have seen and important ways in which the set was used. You might want to consider key moments such as the play's beginning or ending, the first entrance of an important character or the play's climax.

2 Write a paragraph explaining the effect on the audience of this use of set. For example:

> At the end of the play, a trapdoor lowered Faustus out of the audience's view. This was a startling moment for the audience as we realised he was descending to hell. The slow speed of his descent made the tension drawn out and eerie. The effect was heightened by the **wind machines** in the **wings** which blew the pages from Faustus' books in a chaotic swirl. The books, which appeared leather-bound with pages of **parchment**, represented Faustus' lifetime of learning. As the pages flew off the stage and into the audience, it showed that all of that would disappear with him.

THEATRE IN PRACTICE

Es Devlin, from her speech at FutureFest 2016:

I am a set designer. I design stages, spaces where people play, I make space in which people sing. They dance. They speak. They perform plays, songs, and operas. I practise in spaces of all sizes, from 200 people watching Brian Friel's play at the Donmar Warehouse last month to 20,000 people who'll be watching Adele sing on Monday at Madison Square Garden in New York ... Most of my experiences is with **aperture** and frames, I frame people ...

▲ *Es Devlin with her Christmas tree design for the V&A.*

 TIP

You could watch Es Devlin's full speech from FutureFest 2016 on YouTube. She discusses creating 'frames' for the actors. Consider how the set you are analysing contains or enhances the work of the performers. Think about doorways, windows, walls and other framing devices.

 TIP

Consider the shapes and forms used on the stage. There is a difference between the effect of a cube and a circle or a straight line and a squiggle. Consider why a designer has chosen one shape or form over another.

 THEATRE IN PRACTICE

In an article in *The Stage* in 2020, designer Rosie Elnile explained how she sees design as a political act and considers the communities the theatre serves, the ecology of the proposed design and where and how the materials are manufactured. She created a speculative design project which explored planting a garden in the Gate Theatre. Elnile believes, 'Sets are active spaces for acts of transformation.'

▲ *Rosie Elnile's* Prayer *was conceived not as a normal set, but an environment.*

 TIP

When studying the design of a play, explore whether there are cultural and political choices in that design, for example with the types of material used, its relationship to the audience or its relevance to a historical or present political concern. Consider how these choices work with the artistic intentions of the production.

Set design evaluation

Beyond describing and analysing the set, you must judge whether or not it was effective and successful. This means doing more than just expressing that it was 'good' or 'bad' or 'beautiful' or 'ugly'. Think about:

Did the set fulfil its purpose?
For example, if it was meant to represent a certain period or location, did it do that successfully?

Was the set of a high technical standard?
For example, were set changes achieved efficiently and smoothly? Was the set sturdy enough for the demands put on it? Did it suit the staging configuration and avoid blocking sightlines?

Did the set engage and interest the audience?
For example, was it eye-catching or versatile or clever or believable?

Did the set contribute to the mood and atmosphere?
For example, if the play was comic or frightening, did the set contribute to that?

Did the set help you to understand the characters and their lives?
For example, if the characters were wealthy or poverty-stricken, did the set represent that?

Did the set support the action of the play?
For example, if a character was meant to be hidden, did the set create a believable hiding place? If a character made an important entrance, how did the set allow that?

Did the set support the themes of the play?
For example, if the play was about ambition or injustice, did the set convey that?

Sample analysis and evaluation

The following two extracts are from candidate-style responses that analyse and evaluate a set design.

 TIP

These extracts are based on particular candidates' experience of certain performances. They are only example points that could be made, not model answers. Even if you saw the same performance, your recollection, notes and reactions will be different.

TASK 5

1 Read the sample responses and put:
   ▸ **D** next to any performance details
   ▸ **T** next to any correct terminology.
2 Note any points which you believe are analysis (**A**) of the set and any which you would consider evaluation (**E**).
   Examples of each have been done for you.

Approaching Empty at the Kiln Theatre had a largely naturalistic set designed by Rosa Maggiora. It is set in April 2013, immediately after the death of Margaret Thatcher. The set, in an **end on** configuration, **T** represented the office of a struggling minicab company in a northern city. Centre stage were two scuffed inexpensive wood-effect office desks, with office chairs on casters. The desks were cluttered with telephones, tissues, work lamps and stationery. Stage left was a doorway which led to a coffee machine illuminated with a 'Gold Blend' logo light. **D** Stage right was a filing cabinet with an old TV on top, allowing Mansha, the protagonist, to watch the news. The most noticeable aspect of the set, and the one area of stylisation, was the oversized road map (mainly black and white) which covered the entire upstage wall. While difficult to read from the audience, it would seem to show the areas where the cabs go, with bright red lines separating the different districts. The effect was dominant and oppressive, **E** as if there was little to the characters' lives except this scruffy office and the minicabs' routes. **A**

At the heart of the play is the conflict between Mansha and his best friend Raf who runs the business. Both men are from Pakistan and have a shared history, but very different attitudes. Their use of the stage space emphasised these differences, with Mansha sitting comfortably at his desk for most of the play, while Raf rarely sat (his desk faced Mansha's). Instead, he would hastily hang up his coat on the upstage hook, and pace around the stage. In this claustrophobic space, the coffee machine, in a dark space outside the main door, provides a place of escape. When Mansha decides to improve the office, a large can of magnolia paint appears, but, as a sign of the hopelessness of his plans, it just sits in front of a desk, never used. As an audience member, I felt as trapped in the forlorn office as the characters.

The designer attempted to provide an insight into the lives of characters rarely seen on stage. From the handwritten notes on the upstage wall saying 'Rent days are Mondays' and 'Please clean up after your shift', to the small 'luxuries' like a dartboard and a few magazines, the daily grind of struggling workers is depicted. This isn't a beautiful set and at times it was almost difficult to look at, but the choices felt authentic.

B

For *Amadeus* at the National Theatre, the designer Chloe Lamford combined the 18th-century Vienna of Salieri and Mozart with the present day. At the play's opening, the set is being prepared as if a modern concert will begin. It is only when Salieri appears in a period wooden wheelchair **D** that it is clear we are in an earlier time. However, the mixing of period and contemporary features, such as a modern cardboard cake box alongside the many 18th-century period props and architectural features, **A** creates an otherworldly quality, suitable for this memory play. **E**

The key features of the set, on the large **amphitheatre**-style Olivier stage, were several long steps, which led to an upper platform, and columns on either side of this. **T** These had a marble-effect, some apparently three-dimensional and others two dimensional, to suggest the grandeur of the court, but also to draw attention to the artificial and stylised aspects of the design. Gold **candelabras** formed from cherubs heightened the impression of wealth. This supports the action of the play, as we see Salieri gain more wealth as Mozart becomes poorer.

One of the most spectacular uses of the stage was in the presentation of the operas. Elaborate printed **backdrops** provided a magical, playful background. These theatrical interludes had stylised, artificial effects like the man-in-the-moon painted on the backdrop, fluffy clouds and period fanlights. These scenes created excitement for the audience while giving an impression of Mozart's daring and talent.

In contrast, there were several intimate scenes, where props and furnishings were important. In the scene where Salieri tries to seduce Constanza, she often keeps the large centre-stage piano between them and clutches the leather manuscript case to her chest. In other scenes, Mozart is seen on top of the piano. Significantly, when he is in despair, he is on the piano being turned by the ensemble, and papers are scattered across the stage to show the disarray of his life. It is **symbolic** that Mozart is so frequently seen at the piano and, ultimately, it is the location of his death. However, after Mozart's tragic, early death, the designer, through the use of special effects such as gold confetti, celebrates his lasting genius.

The wide variety of design techniques created a great deal of visual interest and surprise. The unpredictability of the mixture of contemporary and period and realistic and stylised, created a heightened theatrical experience which was exciting to experience.

TASK 6

1 Choose a set design from a play you have seen and answer the following question:

> Analyse and evaluate how the set design in the production contributes to the action of the play.

2 Then annotate your answer in the same way as the answers above for detail, terminology, analysis and evaluation.

TIP

Part of the evaluation can be your particular reactions to the set. These may be individual to you, but should be based on your experience as a thoughtful, well-informed audience member.

TASK 7

Choose one of the questions below and make a detailed plan for how you would answer it:

> **a** Evaluate the contribution the set design made to the artistic intentions of the live production, and explain its impact on you as an audience member.
>
> **b** Describe how the set design in two key scenes contributed to the context and mood. Analyse and evaluate how successful it was in communicating meaning to the audience.

TIP

You can use the acronym DATE to check your work:

Details
Analysis
Terminology
Evaluation.

▶ Advice on how to make plans can be found on pages 66–67 in this book.

CHAPTER 5

ANALYSING AND EVALUATING COSTUMES

Costume design is one of the most notable elements of a theatrical production and involves everything characters wear on stage. When writing about it, you can consider many elements such as clothing, accessories, make-up, hairstyles and masks.

Styles of costume

When you first observe the costumes, you should consider what type of costumes they are. They might be, for example:

naturalistic   stylised or fantasy   period or historical

modern contemporary

a combination

The genre, style and setting of the production will dictate the type of costumes employed. Here are some key features of each type.

Naturalistic costumes

These will accurately represent what a character of a certain background at a certain time and place would wear. They will have realistic details. Naturalistic designers work on creating outfits with authenticity. They often give attention to undergarments and the condition of the clothing as well as recreating fabrics and accessories which would have been available in the period or location.

Stylised and fantasy costumes

Stylised costumes do not aim to represent what people actually wear. They tend to emphasise some aspect of the costumes or make a statement about the characters or the world they live in. They may be extreme in shape or style, or present an idealised version of beauty, or could involve **colour-coding** or unusual materials.

▲ Swept

Fantasy costumes are unrealistic and heightened, perhaps suggesting fairy tales or other imaginary worlds. Costumes for a pantomime, for example, often use bright colours and exaggerated silhouettes. Costumes in which actors play animals will be stylised, perhaps by employing a single object like a headpiece, or fantasy, when a full animal body suit might be used.

Modern and contemporary costumes

These costumes reflect what people wear in the present day. They may observe current fashion trends or portray class or geographical differences. They may replicate uniforms, such as those worn by soldiers, school students, doctors or waiters. In some cases, these are bought from workwear stores or second-hand shops. Sometimes a designer will choose to use **modern dress** for a period production, for example, updating a Shakespeare play to the present day.

Historic and period costumes

Historic costumes represent clothing from a period in the past, such as the late-17th-century Puritan community of *The Crucible*, or working-class Salford in the 1950s for *A Taste of Honey*. As such, they will be naturalistic in style. Authentic period costumes often involve a great deal of research. Designers will strive to get details precisely right, including particular fabrics or shoe styles.

Costumes that combine styles

Some designers choose to combine elements of two or more types of costume. For example, the costumes of the leading characters in the musical *Hamilton* are mainly based on historic outfits, while the ensemble costumes suggest the period, but are more stylised, with leggings and bare arms, linking to the modern features of the play. In the original production of *Equus*, the main actors wore naturalistic modern clothing while the horse characters wore stylised metal headpieces and 'hooves'. Some productions have one basic costume to which actors might add a symbolic accessory or item of clothing.

▲ Hedda Gabler

TASK 1

1 Look at the photographs on these pages and decide what types of costume they show.

2 Choose one of the costumes and describe it in as much detail as you can. Consider:

▶ the colours, fabrics and materials used

▶ fit and silhouette

▶ **trim** or other finishings, such as buttons, bows or embroidery

▶ make-up and hairstyles

▶ accessories or other distinctive features.

▲ The Gift of Winter

Drama terminology: costumes

In order to write accurately about costume design, you need to understand the correct terminology.
Below are some useful words to help you describe and analyse what you have seen.

MASKS

Full-face or partial, mime, masque ball, animal.

WIGS

Natural, period or theatrical.

NECKLINE/COLLAR

High, low, scooped; v-neck, turtleneck; Peter Pan, Nehru and so on.

HAIR

Colour, length, style.

JEWELLERY

Earrings, necklace, watch, bracelets, rings, brooches.

HEADWEAR

Hat, scarf, crown, headband, ribbon, headpiece, tiara and so on.

HOSIERY

Tights, stockings, socks; plain or patterned; skin-tone or coloured.

UNDERGARMENTS

Corsetry (such as bras and girdles), underskirts/petticoats, slips, camisoles, briefs.

CONDITION

'Distressed' to look worn or old; pressed, clean, soiled, ripped, stained, mended, faded.

SILHOUETTE AND FIT

Tight, loose, oversized, high waisted, drop waist, hourglass and so on.

FACIAL HAIR

Moustache, sideburns, beards.

PADDING

Protective padding, character padding (for example to make a character rounder), fashion padding (such as shoulder pads), to give a different silhouette.

MAKE-UP

Natural, character, stylised or fantasy.

DECORATIONS AND TRIM

Sequins, rhinestones and so on; buttons, braid, lace, embroidery, faux fur.

NECKWEAR

Ties, scarves, cravats. Wool, silk, polyester, pattern or plain, tied or loose.

COLOUR-CODING

Using certain colours to convey specific meanings, such as social class or membership of a group.

OUTERWEAR

Coats, jackets, capes, shawls, trench coats.

COLOUR PALETTE

The range of colours used, such as muted tones, autumn tones, primary colours, black and white; complementary or clashing.

FABRICS

Silk, wool, cotton, polyester, chiffon, rubber; print or plain.

FOOTWEAR EMBELLISHMENTS

Logos, buckles, charms, straps, ribbons.

FOOTWEAR

Brogues, slip-ons, lace-ups, trainers, heels, slippers, boots and so on.

TASK 2

Write a description of a costume you have seen using at least five of the terms given here.

A downloadable version is available at illuminatepublishing.com.

Making costume notes on the production you have seen

Use the outline and prompts below to make notes on the costumes you saw.
Make your notes as soon as you can after seeing the play.

COSTUME SKETCH AND DESIGN NOTES: DETAILS AND TERMINOLOGY

COSTUME TYPES

Naturalistic?

Stylised?

Fantasy?

Period?

Contemporary?

FIT, SILHOUETTE AND CONDITION

Loose or tight?

High or low waisted?

Narrow or wide shoulders?

Neckline?

Length?

Wrinkled or pressed?

New or old?

Soiled or clean?

HAIR AND MAKE-UP

Wigs or natural?

Long or short?

Colour?

Style?

Natural or exaggerated?

Any features emphasised?

Accessories

Headwear?

Handbags?

Shawls, capes or coats?

Jewellery?

FOOTWEAR

Shoes?

Sandals?

Lace-ups?

Trainers?

Boots?

Barefoot?

COLOURS, FABRICS AND MATERIALS

What are the main colours used?

Are the fabrics plain or patterned?

What textures do the fabrics have?

COSTUME CHANGES

More than one costume?

How were changes achieved?

You may wish to print out more than one of these sheets to analyse different costumes.

How are costumes used?

As you watch the play, think how the costumes contribute to characterisation, style and action. For example:

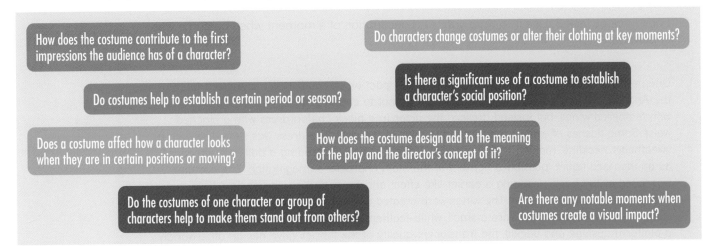

How does the costume contribute to the first impressions the audience has of a character?

Do characters change costumes or alter their clothing at key moments?

Is there a significant use of a costume to establish a character's social position?

Do costumes help to establish a certain period or season?

Does a costume affect how a character looks when they are in certain positions or moving?

How does the costume design add to the meaning of the play and the director's concept of it?

Do the costumes of one character or group of characters help to make them stand out from others?

Are there any notable moments when costumes create a visual impact?

Special costume design challenges

Some costume designers face particular challenges. These may be, for example, the common problems of creating an expensive appearance on a limited budget, or needing quick costume changes; or the particular demands of a script, including recreating animals or unusual beings, such as in Kneehigh Theatre's *Midnight Pumpkin*. Consider if any of the following challenges were met by the designer in the production you saw:

▶ rapid costume changes, occurring either on or off stage

▶ spectacular costumes, possibly very expensive or made on a budget

▶ costumes to create the appearance of non-human creatures

▶ costumes which radically alter the appearance of the actor, for example making them appear much larger

▶ costumes which create an effect when the actor moves, such as long **trains** to dresses, or skirts or capes

▶ costumes which reflect several time periods.

Think about how the designer overcame such challenges. For example, did they use padding to alter the shape of an actor, or use trims, such as faux fur, to give the appearance of wealth? How successful were these choices?

 TIP

Try to find photographs of the production in order to remind yourself of key costume elements.

TASK 3

Recall a play you have seen and important ways in which costumes were used. Use the mind map below to begin developing your ideas:

Impact on audience/me

Moment 1

KEY COSTUME MOMENTS

Impact on audience/me

Moment 2

Impact on audience/me

Hair/make-up/accessories:

Moment 3

Costume description (main outfit):

Hair/make-up/accessories:

Costume description (main outfit):

Hair/make-up/accessories:

Costume description (main outfit):

The response below describes one unusual costume.

TASK 4

1 In the following response, note costume details and the effects of these.
2 Look back at Task 3. Use it to write your own description of a moment when costume was important.

One moment where a costume had a significant impact on the audience was the entrance of the Angel at the end of Act 1. The designer chose not to create a stereotypical angel in white with feathered wings, but instead dressed the actor in a black chiffon dress with a cinched waist. Some flashes of white appeared in the folds of the skirt. The dress was sleeveless with a **sweetheart neckline**, making it glamorous as if the Angel was attending a ball. She appeared as an idealised figure, possibly a figment of the main character's imagination. The costume was laced at the back, providing a corset-like effect and suggested an earlier time than the 1980s in which the play is set. The wings were created with stiff folds of clear cellophane, which shimmered in the light. She wore a small, white-feathered headdress. As she appeared high on a platform upstage and backlit, the translucent quality of the fabrics gave her an otherworldly quality, evoking gasps from the audience.

 THEATRE IN PRACTICE

In an interview for the *LA Times*, Paul Tazewell, the costume designer for *Hamilton*, talks about the process of creating modern and period costumes for the hip-hop musical about the founding fathers of America:

'The first eureka came through the budget limitations imposed by the Public Theater readings. To show the first audiences how the two eras would meet in the look of the show, Tazewell started with a simple parchment-toned silhouette of vest, breeches and boots that then gave way to the blue coats, red trim and brass buttons of Washington's Continental Army. Most important, no wigs.

The success of the workshop resulted in two guiding principles: First, period from the neck down and modern from the neck up; and second, strip away all the embroidered detail of the 18th century so the audience could move past the distraction of artifice to the story itself.'

 THEATRE IN PRACTICE

Nicky Gillibrand, Costume Designer on *The Duchess of Malfi* at the Almeida Theatre (in *The Stage*):

The **Jacobean revenge tragedy** has been cut … and is in modern dress. 'The play feels very current,' Gillibrand says, 'so I'm trying to find pieces that indicate a historical quality. Everyone is in evening wear. Rebecca [Frecknell, the director] used the word "**couture**" and she wanted quite a limited palette, so we've ended up with tones of black and white, and then flesh tones, which in itself is quite challenging. I am trying to describe the Italian court with the choices I make, and push the design so it has a wealthy quality about it, from the Duchess and her brothers, trickling down to the rest of the court.'

Costume evaluation

Beyond describing and analysing the costumes, you must judge whether
or not they were effective and successful. This means doing more than just
commenting that they were 'good' or 'bad' or 'beautiful' or 'ugly'. Think about:

Did the costumes fulfil their purposes?
For example, if they were meant to be from a certain period or location,
did they achieve that?

Did the costumes help you to understand the characters?
For example, if the characters were wealthy or struggling or young or
attention-seeking, did the costumes show that?

Were the costumes of a high technical standard?
For example, could the actors move well in the costumes
and were costume changes achieved efficiently?

Did the costumes provide interest for the audience?
For example, were they eye-catching or versatile or clever or highly appropriate?

Did the costumes contribute to mood and atmosphere?
For example, if the play was meant to be comic or frightening, did costumes add to that?

Did the costumes assist the action of the play?
For example, if a character underwent a change or made an important
entrance, did the costumes support that?

Did the costumes reflect the themes of the play?
For example, if the play was about poverty or ambition, did the costumes convey that?

Sample analysis and evaluation

The following two extracts are from candidate-style responses that analyse and evaluate a costume design.

TIP

These extracts are based on particular candidates' experience of certain performances. They are only example points that could be made, not model answers. Even if you saw the same performance, your recollection, notes and reactions will be different.

TASK 5

1 Read the sample responses and put:

▶ **D** next to any performance details

▶ **T** next to any correct terminology.

2 Note any points which you believe are analysis (**A**) of the set and any which you would consider evaluation (**E**).

One example of each has been done for you.

In *Amadeus*, the costume designer conveyed two periods, 18th-century Vienna and the present day. The latter was mainly represented by the two assistants and the musicians, dressed in contemporary black clothing. In contrast, the main characters wore elaborate period clothing. **T** Salieri's costumes often suggested his wealth, using rich fabrics such as velvet, silk and satin, whose sheen caught the lights. First seen as an older man in a robe of dark purple and gold, with a quilted collar and cuffs, when he suddenly becomes young, a period wig is added. Other bewigged characters in period costumes enter, demonstrating that we are going back in Salieri's memory. His 'younger' costume consists of a frock coat in green, a waistcoat, a white lace collar and gold buttons, embroidery and embellishments. **D** He wears white stockings and heeled shoes adorned with bows. The effect is very much someone of the court intent on making an impression. **A** The green of his frock coat may also hint at the jealousy he expresses in the play. This use of costumes cleverly assists the actor's transformation from dying old man to young ambitious musician. **E**

Mozart's costumes also indicate several aspects of his character. His pastel palette of pinks and yellows suggest his youthful, playful nature. Instead of typical 18th-century court shoes, he wears Doc Marten style boots in a soft pink leather – a modern and **anachronistic** touch that connects him to rebels of a more recent time. However, at the end of the play, when Salieri has destroyed his finances and he is dying, the condition of Mozart's clothes represent how far he has fallen. They are dishevelled, threadbare and stained, contributing to the pity that the audience feels at his death. The paleness of his hair and costumes give him an almost angelic effect, which works well with the Requiem that is played.

B

In *Approaching Empty*, the costumes are all highly naturalistic, like those that could be seen in almost any urban UK location in the early 21st century. The clothing suits British weather: characters are often in jackets, jumpers or coats. In her entrance, Sameena, the young driver, wears warm and practical clothes for her job: a hip-length purple waterproof jacket, black trousers and flat black ankle boots. The fabrics appear to be mainly man-made, such as polyester. Her hair is pulled up into a simple, high ponytail. There are also small indications of her interest in her appearance. She has dark eye shadow. Under her jacket, she wears a knitted pink top with three buttons at its scooped neck. In a later scene, she changes into an orange T-shirt and trainers. Her costumes suggest that she doesn't have much money to spend on clothes, but she is neat and not afraid to wear bright colours.

Mansha, her boss, dresses in a more anonymous way: an inexpensive bland-coloured cardigan with a light shirt underneath, and slip-on shoes. He has wire-rimmed glasses. While Mansha wears comfortable light-coloured clothes, Raf wears darker, more business-like clothing, including a dark overcoat. This light/dark colour-coding may be an indication of the differences between the former best friends. Nothing in Mansha's appearance suggests more than a practical approach to his clothing and shows how he has settled into middle age. A different effect is created when Sameena's villainous brother enters. Dressed in a sharp, well-fitted ensemble of dark coat and trousers, he wears a gold chain, indicating his wealth from his illegal deals. His short hair, beard and false smile add to the ominous effect. We could not mistake that he was a frightening figure.

TASK 6

1 Choose a costume from a play you have seen and answer the following question:

> Analyse and evaluate one costume in the production and explain how it supports the audience's understanding of the character.

2 Then annotate your answer in the same way as the answers above for detail, terminology, analysis and evaluation.

TIP

Part of the evaluation can be your particular reactions to the costumes. These may be individual to you, but should be based on your experience as a thoughtful, well-informed audience member.

TASK 7

Choose one of the questions below and make a detailed plan on how you would answer it:

> a Evaluate how the costume design supported the genre or style of the production and the impact it had on you as an audience member.
>
> b Describe how the costume designer used one costume to contribute to the meaning and themes of the play. Analyse and evaluate how successful they were in communicating meaning to the audience.

TIP

You can use the acronym DATE to check your work:

Details
Analysis
Terminology
Evaluation.

▶ **For more advice on how to create plans, go to pages 66–67 of this book.**

CHAPTER 6

ANALYSING AND EVALUATING LIGHTING

Lighting can significantly affect an audience's experience of a play. Lighting design involves choosing the types of lighting and their intensity, angles and colour, as well as deciding how the lighting will serve the style and meaning of the play. It can include elements such as **transitions** and special effects.

Lighting styles

When you first consider the lighting, think about the desired effects and the type of lighting design it is. It might be, for example:

naturalistic

minimalist

stylised

a combination of lighting types

The genre and style of the production will influence the type of lighting used. Here are some key features of each type.

Naturalistic lighting

This lighting will have realistic details and the design may accurately recreate the lighting of a certain place or period. A play set in a 1950s house, for example, may use some **practical** 1950s floor or table lamps, and the actors will give the appearance of turning them on and off. A play set in a factory may have fluorescent **strip lights** to replicate the harsh lighting of that setting. Some period plays may use real or imitation candles or period lanterns.

Theatrical lights will be used to replicate the light available at a certain time of day, season or the location of the scene. For example, the lighting designer may consider the angle and type of light which would pour into a window indicating morning sun or a moonlit sky.

Stylised lighting

This lighting has exaggerated or non-naturalistic features. For example, a **follow-spot** might isolate and highlight a singer, or red coloured **gels** might suggest the theme of violence. Special effects like **strobes** may create heightened effects. The designer may decide to use lighting in an abstract way, for example by using swirling **gobos** to suggest a character's confusion or carefully defined squares of light to show imprisonment.

Minimalist lighting

This type of lighting uses very little technical equipment. There may be only a couple of **lanterns** used and, in some cases, the actors will operate the lighting themselves. Actors may also use torches or other small lighting devices. A minimalist style is often associated with small-scale, low-budget productions or shows where the focus is entirely on the actors and storytelling rather than spectacle.

▲ Coloured strip lights in a student-devised play.

Combination

Some designers choose to combine elements of two or more types of lighting design.

 TIP

Consider the scale and budget of the production you have seen. A small studio production will require very different lighting from a major musical like *Wicked*, for which the original lighting designer, Kenneth Posner, used over 800 individual lights.

TASK 1

1 Look at the photographs below and decide what type of lighting is used in each one.

2 Choose one of the lighting designs and describe it in as much detail as you can. Write about:

▶ the colours and intensity of the lights

▶ the positioning of the lighting (upstage, downstage …) and angles (high, low, diagonal, side …)

▶ equipment likely to be used to create these effects

▶ special effects, such as gobos or a **smoke machine**

▶ other distinctive features, such as shadows or unusual focusing.

▲ Wicked

▲ Blood Play

▲ Animal Crackers

▲ Pink Mist

rama terminology: lighting

order to write accurately about lighting design, you need to understand the correct terminology.
elow are some useful words to help you describe and analyse what you have seen.

WASH
Light which covers the whole stage or large area of it.

DIAGONALS
Lights projected down at roughly a 45-degree angle.

LIGHTING RIG
The structure that holds the lighting equipment in the theatre.

SPOTLIGHT
A lamp that projects a bright light onto an area of stage, usually focusing on a performer.

FOLLOW-SPOT
A lamp that produces a bright beam, which can be operated to 'follow' a performer.

LIGHTING PLOT
Similar to an architectural plan, to show where the lights will hang. It shows the position, type of lighting fixture and colours of gels.

HOUSE LIGHTS
The lights in the auditorium that are usually on while the audience is being seated and then dimmed when the performance is about to begin.

LANTERN
A lamp and reflector in a box which produces lighting. There are different types of lantern, such as profile, fresnel and flood.

SMOKE, FOG OR HAZE MACHINE
A piece of equipment which uses a gas to produce clouds or mists.

LED LIGHTS
Powerful and colourful lights that don't require gels and are energy efficient.

FOOTLIGHTS
Low lights placed on the downstage edge. Popular in Victorian theatres and sometimes now used to create period lighting effects.

TASK 2

Write a description of a lighting design you have seen. Use at least five of the terms given here.

DOWNLIGHT OR TOP-LIGHT

Light from directly overhead.

STROBE

A lighting device that gives short, bright bursts of bright light.

FILTER OR GEL

A coloured piece of plastic inserted into a case on a lantern to alter the colour of the light.

GOBO

A metal, glass or plastic cut-out attached to a lantern to project patterns, such as leaves, stars, swirls or waves.

BLACKOUT

Switching off all stage lights. This can be sudden or gradual.

CUE TIMING

The time it takes for a lighting change, for example the counts until a blackout occurs or how long a cross-fade takes.

PRACTICAL LIGHTS

Working onstage lights that are used in the set, such as desk lamps, torches or candles.

PYROTECHNICS

Special effects that create dramatic effects, such as fireworks, explosions or flashes.

BACKLIGHTING

Lighting projected from a source upstage. It highlights the outline of actors or scenery and separates them from the background.

FADE

Gradually bring up or diminish lights.

MOVING LIGHT

Either a lighting fixture moved manually by an operator, or a computer-operated fixture which is moved remotely.

FLOOR LIGHTING

Lanterns placed on low stands, often used to cast shadows.

A downloadable version is available at illuminatepublishing.com.

TIP

If you can, find photographs of the production to remind yourself of key elements of the lighting.

Making lighting notes on the production you have seen

Use the mind map below to make notes on the show you have seen. The prompts are suggestions to aid you, but won't cover every feature. You will probably find it useful to draw a sketch of the stage at each key lighting moment.

Ideally, make your notes as soon as you can after seeing the play.

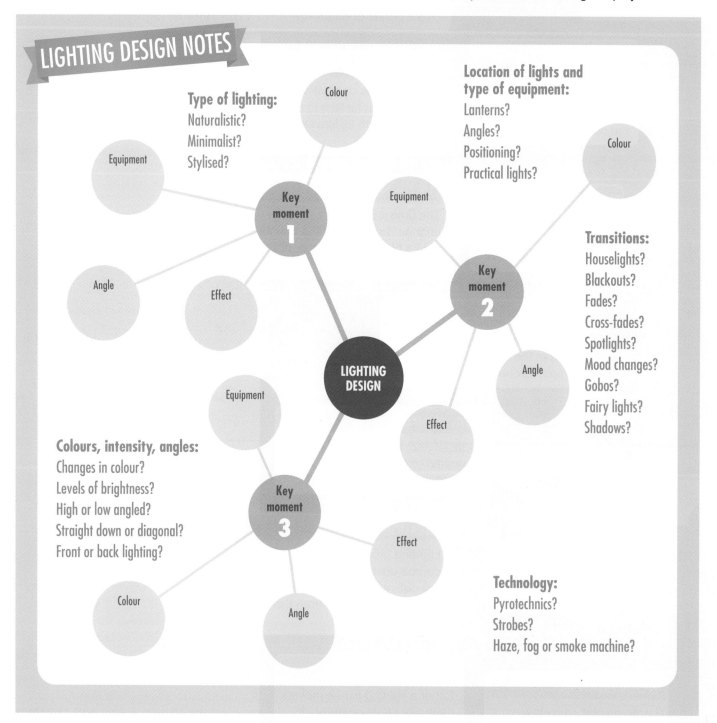

LIGHTING DESIGN NOTES

Type of lighting:
Naturalistic?
Minimalist?
Stylised?

Colour

Equipment

Angle

Effect

Key moment 1

Location of lights and type of equipment:
Lanterns?
Angles?
Positioning?
Practical lights?

Equipment

Colour

Key moment 2

Angle

Effect

Transitions:
Houselights?
Blackouts?
Fades?
Cross-fades?
Spotlights?
Mood changes?
Gobos?
Fairy lights?
Shadows?

LIGHTING DESIGN

Equipment

Colours, intensity, angles:
Changes in colour?
Levels of brightness?
High or low angled?
Straight down or diagonal?
Front or back lighting?

Key moment 3

Effect

Colour

Angle

Technology:
Pyrotechnics?
Strobes?
Haze, fog or smoke machine?

You may wish to print out more than one of these sheets to analyse different moments.

How is the lighting used?

As you watch the play, consider different ways in which the lighting contributes to the mood and action of the play. For example:

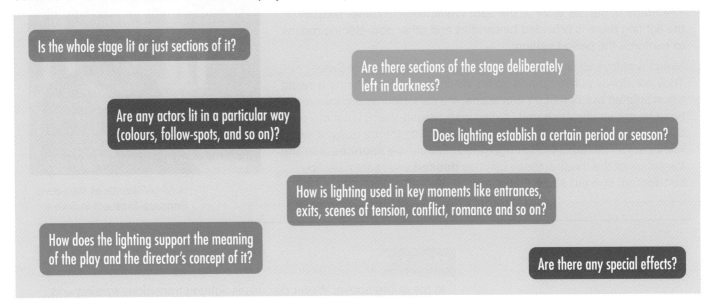

Is the whole stage lit or just sections of it?

Are there sections of the stage deliberately left in darkness?

Are any actors lit in a particular way (colours, follow-spots, and so on)?

Does lighting establish a certain period or season?

How is lighting used in key moments like entrances, exits, scenes of tension, conflict, romance and so on?

How does the lighting support the meaning of the play and the director's concept of it?

Are there any special effects?

Lighting effects

Many plays use lighting to create a special effect or reinforce a theme of a play. The fairy lights and green **LEDs** used in *Wicked* set up the fantastical Emerald City for the audience. The **backlighting** in *Coriolanus* when Coriolanus showers, emphasises the impact of the water on his wounds and his pain, as well as creating a beautiful effect with the translucent splashes of water. In the musical *Six*, about the wives of Henry VIII, each queen has her own shape on the back wall made up of LED lights to emphasise her identity.

 TIP

You might not be able to identify the precise lighting equipment used in a production, but you may well see the angles and locations of lights. For example, front lights provide visibility, but used alone can flatten an image. Side or **diagonal** lights can add more shaping for a more three-dimensional or sculptural effect, and backlighting is good for emphasising an outline or silhouette.

TASK 3

1 Recall a play you have seen and any important ways in which the lighting was used to reinforce a theme or support meaning.

2 Write a paragraph explaining the effect of this use of lighting. For example:

In this production, which shows the darker side of life in an American high school, the lighting designer used bright, clean, colourful LED **washes** for the more upbeat scenes. To further emphasise the school setting, LEDs, in what looked like old-fashioned fluorescent strip lights, were hung from the ceiling of the set. For the prom, moving gobos created a disco-ball effect. In the contrasting sections where the protagonist directly addressed the audience, a sharp-edged spotlight cast a harsh white circular pattern around him. When he was speaking, the rest of the stage was shadowy, with blue gels creating an ominous feeling. The combination of the bright high school lights with the darker **direct address** sections captures the two sides of high school life.

THEATRE IN PRACTICE

Lighting designer Prema Mehta was interviewed by Kate Wyver in *The Stage* about her work at the Sam Wanamaker Theatre. Most of the lighting there is provided by candles and other non-electric means to reinforce the period setting:

Mehta employs all six of the Wanamaker's candelabras for *Swive*. They are slowly pulled up and down, spinning like an unwinding swing when snuffed out or relit. In one scene, the candelabras are lowered to head height as Elizabeth and Dudley walk among them. 'That intimacy of looking at each other through the candles was for me quite striking,' Mehta says, 'beautifully choreographed.' Six candle **sconces** also line the pillars of the theatre, these candles **doused** and reanimated by soft-footed, hooded stage managers.

▲ *Nina Cassells as the young Princess Elizabeth in* Swive.

TASK 4

In the quote above, Wyver discusses lighting transitions (raising and lowering candelabras; candles lit and extinguished by stage managers). Can you think of any notable lighting transitions, such as **blackouts**, **fades**, or **cross-fades**, in the production you saw? Explain how the transitions help the audience to understand the action of the play.

 THEATRE IN PRACTICE

Tim Deiling, designer of *Six* and winner of Young Designer of the Year, in *City Theatrical*:

'Some designers have a spectacular singular **aesthetic** that works really well and you can always spot one of their shows out in the crowd. Often to stunning results. The danger here however is the show needs to suit them and not the other way around. I try my best to serve the piece and not myself. I have the most respect for designers with range who can deliver a lush opera one day, a big musical the next, and trendy play after. Sometimes ego and ambition need to take a back seat to the practical needs of the play. And yet … the punters still need value for money. Personally, I don't have much interest in realism in theatre. For me good theatre is **expressionistic**, it's high contrast, a heightened reality to convey a point. My lighting tries always to reflect that where appropriate.'

 TIP

One job of the lighting designer is to help focus the audience's attention on a character or part of the stage. This might be done in many ways, including the use of follow-spots, changes in colour or fading lights up or down. As you recall productions you have seen, think of moments where the lighting drew you to look at something in particular.

Lighting evaluation

Beyond describing and analysing the lighting, you must judge
whether or not it was effective and successful. This means
doing more than just expressing that it was 'good' or 'bad'
or 'beautiful' or 'ugly'. Think about:

Did the lighting fulfil its purpose?
Were the actors and set appropriately lit so that they could be seen as intended? Did
lighting help to present a location or period? Did cues take place when they should have?

Was the lighting of a high technical standard?
For example, were changes accomplished smoothly? Were blackouts efficient? Did the
timing of changes seem correct? Was the lighting effective within the staging configuration?

Did the lighting engage and interest the audience?
For example, was it eye-catching or versatile or highly appropriate?

Did lighting contribute to mood and atmosphere?
For example, if the play was comic or frightening or romantic, did the lighting match that?

Did lighting enhance your understanding of the characters?
Were you able to follow the lead actors? If a character's home or
costumes were meant to be luxurious, did the lighting contribute to that?

Did lighting help to convey the action of the play?
For example, if something magical was meant to happen, did the lighting
achieve that? If an entrance was important, did the lighting support it?

Did the lighting reinforce the themes of the play?
For example, if the play was about violence, magic, poverty or love, did the lighting convey that?

TIP

These extracts are based on particular candidates' experience of certain performances. They are only example points that could be made, not model answers. Even if you saw the same performance, your recollection, notes and reactions will be different.

Sample analysis and evaluation

The following two extracts are from candidate-style responses that analyse and evaluate lighting design.

TASK 5

1 Read the sample responses and put:

> **D** next to any performance details

> **T** next to any correct terminology.

2 Note any points which you believe are analysis (**A**) of the lighting and any which you would consider evaluation (**E**).

Examples of each have been done for you.

Paule Constable has cleverly **E** used her lighting design to recreate how Christopher's brain works in *The Curious Incident of the Dog in the Night-Time*. The stylised lighting constantly, and quickly, changes. The colours are primarily white or blue-ish, **D** suggesting a certain coldness and control. **A** Christopher is frequently seen in a white round spotlight, **T** which focuses the audience on him as the play's protagonist and suggests that he is separate from others.

In the busy train-station scene, the lights are constantly moving, and projections with words on them roll along the floor, suggesting the sensory overload caused by that unfamiliar location. As he is on his journey, Christopher is always lit, while members of the ensemble are frequently in shadows. This is particularly noticeable when he is lifted by the ensemble while he appears to float above them, creating a beautiful and moving image.

When Christopher is problem-solving, the lights reinforce this. At one point, I noticed that a box would light up and Christopher would approach it, showing him travelling from one idea to another. At another point, red lights were dotted on the grid of the stage, reflecting Christopher's mathematical ability and how his brain quickly makes connections.

My favourite use of lighting was in the letter scene, when low-angled lights illuminate the letters that Christopher and the ensemble are holding. In addition, Christopher has a practical torch in his mouth which lights the letter in his hand. This creates an unusual **tableau**, focusing the audience on the great importance of Christopher discovering that his mother has been writing to him.

B

The lighting of *Amadeus* supports the theatricality of the play. There are two stages on view – the actual stage and then, upstage, a secondary space where some of the opera performances take place. **Footlights** are arranged around the edge of the main stage. On the upper stage, fanned footlights with an old-fashioned appearance **D** create the sense of a period stage. **A**

Another highly theatrical use of lighting is the backlighting of the ghost from *Don Giovanni*. **T** This otherworldly effect is heightened by the use of a smoke machine. Important colour gels are golden hues – which highlight the richness of the fabrics of the costumes – and blues – which show the darker side of Salieri's memories. These also successfully guide the audience to understanding the time jumps in the play. **E**

Towards the end of the play, the stylised theatricality of the lighting highlights Salieri's descent and Mozart's ultimate success. While only Salieri is lit from the front and side, he is surrounded by backlit, black-clad musicians, while gold confetti rains down on them. This makes Salieri appear to 'pop' out from the others, who are partially in shadows and do not register as individuals, appropriately placing the focus on him. From three sides, sets of layered diagonal lights pour down on Salieri as if conquering him. After his final lines, the lights slowly fade to blackout, leaving the audience to reflect on how Salieri's envy has ultimately led to a wasted life.

TIP

One key area where a lighting design might be criticised is poor timing of cues. Consider if a blackout occurred too quickly or a fade took too long. Did the timing and rhythm of the cues support the action and mood of the play?

TASK 6

1 Choose a lighting design from a play you have seen and answer the following question:

> Analyse and evaluate two key moments from the lighting design in the production and explain how it creates mood and atmosphere for the audience.

2 Then annotate your answer in the same way as the answers above for detail, terminology, analysis and evaluation.

TASK 7

Choose one of the questions below and make a detailed plan on how you would answer it:

a Describe how lighting was used to support the style of the production. Analyse and evaluate how successful the lighting design was in helping to convey the style to the audience.

b Analyse and evaluate the use of lighting in key moments to communicate meaning to the audience.

c Analyse and evaluate how the visual elements of the production, including the lighting, supported the action of the play.

TIP

You can use the acronym DATE to check your work:

Details
Analysis
Terminology
Evaluation.

▶ **For advice on how to create plans, go to pages 66–67 in this book.**

CHAPTER 7

ANALYSING AND EVALUATING SOUND

Sound design is an important element of theatrical production, yet it can be one of the most challenging to write about. Sound design includes any sound effects or music heard on stage. Often the effects are subtle and, although the audience is influenced by them, they may not always be able to explain why.

Many theatre makers feel that sound design should support the show rather than draw attention to itself. One sound designer has said, 'If you come out of a play, commenting about the sound design, I've got it wrong.' On the other hand, some sound designs are very attention-grabbing and may include specially composed music and onstage musicians.

Styles of sound

The types of sound design will vary depending on the demands of the production. The sound might be, for example:

naturalistic

abstract

music-based

a combination of different types of sound

Here are some key features of each type:

Naturalistic sound

This could involve **motivated sounds**, which are sounds indicated in the script, such as gunshots or doorbells. There may also be realistic sounds incorporated to create the setting of the play, such as sound effects of birdsong and cows mooing to establish a rural location, or traffic noises for an urban scene.

Abstract sound

Abstract sounds are not realistic. They may be atmospheric or symbolic. To suggest the passing of time, for example, a sound designer might manipulate the sound of slowly dripping water, or, to create tension, amplify a creaking noise.

Music

This can be an original composition or existing music. Some sound designers use a musical **motif** for certain characters or settings. The music may be performed by musicians on or off stage, or be recorded and played back.

Combination

Frequently, productions will use a combination of music and sound effects. There may even be some recorded music used as well as some played live on stage.

▲ Musicians in the orchestra 'pit' prepare for a production of the musical Cabaret.

TASK 1

Read the descriptions of different sound designs below and decide what types of sound they are.

Set in a mid-20th-century recording studio, the main actress sang a well-known blues song into a microphone, while a trio of musicians played behind her.

To one side, there was a table full of props. The actors took turns to provide live sound effects, including the sound of a horse's hooves by banging two coconut shells together.

Pop songs from the 1990s played in the prom scene.

To create the atmosphere of a busy 1940s newspaper office, there were ringing telephones and clacking typewriters.

Every time Felicity entered, she was accompanied a lyrical motif of piano music.

To show the heroine's mental distress when she was upset, a loud buzzing noise was heard.

The maid answered the telephone when it rang.

To create a frightening atmosphere, there was a recorded sound of a woman laughing which had been treated with a reverb effect so that it echoed ominously.

TASK 2

Consider one or two sound design moments from a production you have seen and write a few detailed sentences about them. Include, for example:

▶ the type of sound it was
▶ whether it was live or recorded
▶ if it was motivated by the script
▶ how it added to the setting of play
▶ how it added to the mood of the play
▶ if it was amplified
▶ the effect created.

Drama terminology: sound

In order to write accurately about sound design, you need to understand the correct terminology. Below are some useful words to help you describe and analyse what you have seen and heard.

VOLUME

How loud or soft a sound or voice is.

SPEAKERS

Means of amplifying and projecting sound. The placement of speakers will influence how the audience experiences the sound.

ACTOR-MUSICIANS

Performers who play musical instruments as part of their acting roles.

MUSICAL INSTRUMENTS

Drums, guitars, violins and so on, which might be played by a band, orchestra or actors.

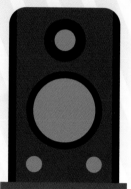

COMPOSER

Someone who writes music. Some productions have a composer to create original music.

SNAP

Turn sound suddenly off or on.

FADE

Gradually turn sound up or down.

REVERB

An echoing effect, sustaining the sound longer than usual.

SOUND EFFECTS

Special sounds created either live or recorded, such as slamming doors or alarm bells.

SCENE CHANGES OR TRANSITIONS

How music or sound is used during transitions or scene changes, often to establish a new location or change in mood.

TASK 3

Write a description of a sound design you have experienced. Use at least five of the terms given here.

MICROPHONES

Devices for converting and amplifying sound, including:
radio mics: portable microphones, often worn, which allow actors and singers to be amplified with no visible means of connection
overheads: microphones hung above the stage to boost the overall sound.

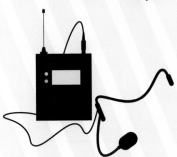

RECORDED SOUND

Sound that has been recorded specially for playback during the performance or selected from sound effects archives.

LIVE SOUND

Sound created by the stage management, technicians or actors during the performance.

PRE-SHOW MUSIC

Music played as the audience enters and waits for the performance to begin.

CURTAIN-CALL MUSIC

Music played during the **curtain call**. Sometimes the curtain call is choreographed to a song.

ACOUSTICS

The sound quality of a given space, including how the size and shape of the theatre affects the warmth or clarity of sound.

A downloadable version is available at illuminatepublishing.com.

Making sound design notes on the production you have seen

Use the chart below to make notes on sound in the show you attended. The prompts are suggestions to aid you, but won't cover every feature.

Ideally, make your notes as soon as you can after seeing the play.

Sound design notes		
Production		
Type of sound	▶ Naturalistic? ▶ Abstract? ▶ Motivated? ▶ Music?	
How the sound is produced	▶ Live or recorded? ▶ Amplified or not? ▶ On stage or off? ▶ Location of speakers? ▶ Snap or fade on and off?	If you notice any microphones or speakers, sketch them here.
Quality and nature of sound	▶ Loud or soft? ▶ Pleasant or **discordant**? ▶ Calm or quick? ▶ Natural or treated (for example, reverb or other distortion)	
Music	▶ Original or existing? ▶ Style? ▶ Instruments? ▶ Period or contemporary?	
Effects of music	▶ Do characters react to music? ▶ How does audience react to music? ▶ Is music linked to a character or event?	
Acoustics	▶ Warm or cold? ▶ Clear or muffled? ▶ Silent surroundings or competing sounds?	

How is sound used?

As you watch the play, consider different ways in which the sound contributes to the mood and action of the play. For example:

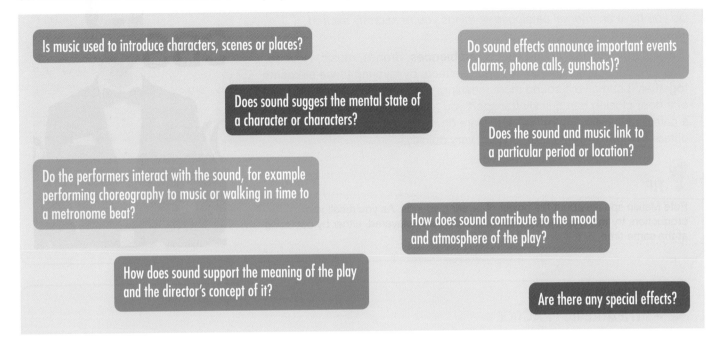

Is music used to introduce characters, scenes or places?

Do sound effects announce important events (alarms, phone calls, gunshots)?

Does sound suggest the mental state of a character or characters?

Does the sound and music link to a particular period or location?

Do the performers interact with the sound, for example performing choreography to music or walking in time to a metronome beat?

How does sound contribute to the mood and atmosphere of the play?

How does sound support the meaning of the play and the director's concept of it?

Are there any special effects?

Significant sound effects

Even in Shakespeare's time, there were some special sound effects, such as using a metal sheet or rolling cannon ball to recreate thunder. Onstage musicians were frequently used, providing fanfares before a royal entrance or a military battle, for example. In contemporary theatre, special effects might include:

▶ underscoring: music played with the action of a scene

▶ explosions

▶ rain and storm effects

▶ soundscapes (layered sounds)

▶ electronic sound effects.

TIP

Consider if the sounds you hear work with the images on the stage or are **contrapuntal**, meaning that they strongly contrast with the image. For example, a sad image might be contrasted with a cheery song.

TASK 4

1 Recall a play you have seen and important ways in which sound was used. You might want to consider key moments such as the play's beginning or ending, the first entrance of an important character or the play's climax.

2 Write a paragraph explaining the effect on the audience of this use of sound. For example:

> The sound design for this production of *Lord of the Flies* was almost entirely abstract and relied on electronic, synthesiser sounds. For example, at the beginning, where you might have expected to hear the noises of a plane in flight and then crashing, instead there was a recorded sound of electronic music, which suggested movement through its rapid beat, without literally sounding like a plane. After about 20 seconds, it reached a **crescendo** of noise, without entirely sounding like a crash. The volume and metallic urgency made it clear that something out of the ordinary was happening, but not what it was. It was only when the boys emerged that we understood what the sounds meant, which I found slightly disappointing.

THEATRE IN PRACTICE

Interview with sound designer Pete Malkin in *Oxford Culture Review*:

Do you have an internal catalogue of things you're secretly excited about using?

'Basic things include: sound effects, **ambiences**, drones, music. I love to create Soundscapes and unique sound effects by layering these elements together, it can give a sound more meaning. For example, the simple sound of a door closing can quickly transport you to a new location, layer this with a café bell, a reloading of a gun, a snare drum, they all give the audience a different context for the new location very quickly.'

TIP

Pete Malkin speaks about the power of layering sounds. As you recall your production, try to think of examples where sounds are layered, either by occurring at the same time, or following in quick succession.

 THEATRE IN PRACTICE

Composer Grant Olding, who wrote the music and performed in the band for *One Man, Two Guvnors* (from the National Theatre learning pack):

What were your initial discussions with the director about the role music would play in One Man, Two Guvnors?

'The first conversations I had with Nick [director Nicholas Hytner] were about time, place and style. He told me it was set in 1963, Brighton, and mentioned Ealing comedies [films from Ealing Studios, 1947–1957], *Carry On* films [low-budget comedies, 1958–1978] and early Beatles music. Later, he abandoned the above in place of skiffle music. Later still, it was Variety acts. Finally, we decided we would make our own rules up and create a **hybrid** of all the styles we wanted to incorporate. Nick began sending me YouTube clips of crazy Variety acts; people playing car horns and xylophones. We decided there would be music in between scenes, but we didn't know if that would just be incidental music, or actual songs, or if there would be underscoring during the actual scenes. Before rehearsals began, we did a workshop and decided the band would be on stage and that would be the skiffle band that the character of Francis mentions in the play.'

How does writing music for plays differ from writing songs for musicals?

'The main difference is that in musical theatre you tend to be in control of the whole show; in plays, you're trying to serve everyone else. In a musical, the emotional journeys and themes, and therefore the structure of the show, are driven by the composer; so you're dictating where the underscore goes, how you're going to get into a song etc. In a play, the director gives you a list of what music they need; for example, scene change music or underscoring. If a scene change takes longer than expected, then they will ask you to write an extra twenty seconds of music. In *One Man, Two Guvnors*, there's only one piece of scene change music which tells you something about the emotion of the characters [the blues music before the pier scene in Act Two].'

 TASK 5

Grant Olding talks about establishing time, place and style through music. Think of a show you have seen and describe how sound contributed to your understanding of its context and style.

▲ *Suzie Toase and James Corden in* One Man, Two Guvnors.

Sound design evaluation

Beyond describing and analysing the sound, you must judge whether or not it was effective and successful. This means doing more than just expressing that it was 'good' or 'bad' or 'beautiful' or 'dull'. Think about:

Did the sound fulfil its purpose?
For example, if it was meant to represent a certain period or location, did it do that successfully?

Was the sound of a high technical standard?
For example, were volume levels appropriate? Were cues completed on time?

Did the sound engage and interest the audience?
For example, was the music catchy, beautiful, memorable or surprising?

Did sound contribute to mood and atmosphere?
For example, if the play was meant to be comic or frightening, did sound add to that?

Did the sound help you to understand the characters?
For example, was music used to introduce a character or to underscore their speech?

Did sound add to the action of the play?
For example, did it help to establish changes in location, time or mood?

Did the sound design support the themes of the play?
For example, if the play was about love, conflict or childhood, did the sound help to convey that?

TIP

These extracts are based on particular candidates' experience of certain performances. They are only example points that could be made, not model answers. Even if you saw the same performance, your recollection, notes and reactions will be different.

TIP

Two elements which are frequently criticised in sound design are volume and timing. Sound designers and technicians must ensure that sound is balanced so that, for example, the lyrics of a song are not drowned out. Similarly, a mistimed cue, like a telephone which carries on ringing after an actor has answered it, can destroy the audience's belief in a moment.

TIP

Part of the evaluation can be your particular reactions to the sound. These may be individual to you, but should be based on your experience as a thoughtful, well-informed audience member.

▲ *Indira Varma as Grace in* Faith Healer.

Sample analysis and evaluation

The following two extracts are from candidate-style responses that analyse and evaluate a sound design.

 TASK 6

1 Read the following sample responses and put:
   - ▶ **D** next to any performance details
   - ▶ **T** next to any correct terminology.

2 Note any points which you believe are analysis (**A**) of the set and any which you would consider evaluation (**E**).

One example of each has been done for you.

A

Although the use of sound in the Old Vic production of *Faith Healer* was minimal, when it was used, it was highly effective. **E** The first sound effect was the ominous drumming of a bodhrán. **D** As this is a well-known type of Irish drum, this prepares the audience for the nationality of Francis Hardy, the faith healer of the title. **A** As he begins to speak, the recorded sound of the drumming continues, underscoring his first lines, and then slowly fades out. **T** After this, there are few sound cues, though Francis does sing bits of an old romantic song at one point and imitates his mother's breathless and warbly singing. However, when he describes meeting the group from the wedding reception in the pub, it is underscored by Irish fiddle music, played at a very low volume, suggesting the sort of party music that would have been at the wedding. This creates a more celebratory mood, very different from the rest of the first scene. But then the music **snaps** off suddenly, leaving the line 'Nothing at all' to be said with only silence behind it. At that moment, the mood turns darker and frightening, appropriate for the sad events that are to follow.

Each of the four monologues that makes up the play is introduced by the drumming, but there are subtle differences in the music in the other scenes. When Grace recalls meeting the wedding guests, the music is primarily Irish pipes or flutes at a slightly louder volume, which snaps off before her line 'That's the curtain raiser,' again creating suspense. For Teddy's scene, the military-type drumming overlaps with an old recording of a Fred Astaire song. Teddy sings along, not very tunefully, remembering it with affection. This particular song is motivated by the script as it is referenced by all the characters, but this is the first time the audience hears it. When Teddy recollects the wedding guests, his speech is underscored by Irish fiddle and pipe music, which sounds romantic and full of longing as he realises his love for Grace and Francis. But when it snaps off, he says, 'Going to cure you of that trouble.' The music snapping off is an excellent example of how silence is as important as sound, as it makes the following line stand out for the audience. The final use of the drum begins with a single low beat as Francis takes his first step towards his death. After silence on the word 'silent,' the drum slowly beats, creating a sense of doom as he walks into the darkness. Throughout the play, the simple but carefully chosen use of music supports the different tales of the characters.

B

Blowin' in the Wind by Chickenshed Theatre Company uses a wide variety of music and sound to convey its theme of the struggle for civil rights. As the audience entered, we heard a live band playing contemporary music, creating a party or club atmosphere. When the music stopped, a sound recording of a Martin Luther King speech began. It was a period recording and had a dated, slightly crackling quality. Another voice eventually overlapped it, amplified by a microphone, issuing instructions on how to get to the march, followed by the audio from an American newscast about the March on Washington. Lastly, a solo female performer appeared on stage and sang the protest song 'Blowin' in the Wind,' again amplified by a microphone. Through the use of sound, and without actual dialogue, the sound designer established both the mood and themes of the play. As audience members, we felt caught up in the protests that were beginning, surrounded by exciting sounds and movement.

A contrasting use of music was the recorded flute and amplified narration about the indigenous people of America while the ensemble performed slow, graceful movements. This music was then layered and eventually overtaken by pulsing drumming and recorded narration. A crashing drum solo introduced the first white settlers. So, music at first established a peaceful mood, which eventually gave way to conflict and violence, with drums and cymbals marking each disaster. This section was less successful to me, as I found the drumming made me miss some of the narration and it became repetitive. However, the sound designer's varied, **montage** approach reinforced the director's concept of a loose, **non-linear** narrative exposing centuries of struggles. Particularly effective was the use of **documentary** sound to capture the actual words of key figures, so as an audience member I felt engaged and informed.

TASK 7

1 Choose a sound design from a play you have seen and answer the following question:

> Analyse and evaluate the sound design in the production and explain how it adds to the mood and meaning of the play for the audience.

2 Then annotate your answer in the same way as the answers above for detail, terminology, analysis and evaluation.

▲ *JoJo Morrall as Rosa Parks wears a radio mic in* Blowin' in the Wind.

TASK 8

Choose one of the questions below and make a detailed plan for how you would answer it:

a Evaluate how the aural aspects supported the genre or style of the production and the impact it had on you as an audience member.

b Describe how sound design supported the action and artistic intentions of the production. Analyse and evaluate how successful the sound design was in helping to convey meaning to the audience.

TIP

You can use the acronym DATE to check your work:
Details
Analysis
Terminology
Evaluation.

▶ Advice on how to make plans can be found on pages 66–67 in this book.

CHAPTER 8

DEVELOPING YOUR WRITING SKILLS

Examiners have highlighted that Drama students often write with great enthusiasm and engagement about the productions they have seen and this is a strength in the Live Theatre responses. The best answers show students' knowledge of theatre and their personal reactions to what they have experienced. However, many students find it a challenge to organise their ideas and make their points within time constraints. The following pages offer suggestions on how to develop these skills.

Reading the question

Carefully read the question and make sure that you answer it precisely. One way to do this is to underline key words and, if they are provided, use the bullet points for extra guidance. For example:

1 How and why certain design choices were made.

2 How successful those choices were.

4 Choose two key scenes, perhaps contrasting.

7 Type of play: naturalistic, stylised, minimalistic, comic, and so on.

9 Mood, emotions, ambience.

Analyse and evaluate how the set design in two key scenes helped to communicate meaning to the audience.

You may consider:

- the style of the production
- how the set design is used to aid the action and atmosphere of the production
- your response to the set design as an audience member.

3 Your focus is set design.

5 The purpose of the play, such as its plot, themes and characters.

6 Impact or effect on audience, including you.

8 Main events, such as moments of conflict or change.

10 Your personal reactions, possibly a cue to write 'I' at certain points.

If you were writing a response to a set design of *A Midsummer Night's Dream*, for example, you might choose two contrasting scenes, perhaps one in the court and one in the forest. You might explain how the set showed the differences between those worlds. You would analyse the set by breaking down elements of it, such as colours, materials, textures and size, and commenting on the effect of those choices. You might look at the period/fantasy styles and how the set reflected the rules of one world and the wildness of the other. You would offer what you thought worked well and what, if anything, could have been better.

TASK 1

1 Look at the questions below and highlight the key words.
2 Write notes on how you could begin to apply those words to an analysis and evaluation of a production you have seen.

AQA

Describe how lighting was used to support the style and context of the production. Analyse and evaluate how successful the lighting design was in engaging the audience.

You should make reference to:

- colours, angles and intensity
- any transitions
- any special effects
- a section of the play or the whole play. [32]

OCR

Analyse how successfully the style or genre of the play was communicated to you by the visual elements in the live performance you have seen.

In your answer, you should consider:

- what you felt the style and genre were
- how effectively the visual elements such as set, lighting and/or costume were used to support the style and genre
- what skills the designers used to create and their impact on you.

You should use appropriate drama and theatre terminology. [30]

WJEC

Analyse and evaluate the use of sound in at least two key moments to communicate meaning to the audience. In your answer, refer to:

- the style of the production
- how sound, including music and special effects, was used
- your response to the sound design as an audience member. [15]

Edexcel

a Analyse how characterisation was used to engage the audience at a climactic moment of the performance. [6]

b Evaluate how the costume design aided characterisation and created impact within the performance. [9]

Eduqas

Analyse and evaluate how vocal skills by an actor in two key scenes created impact for the audience.

In your answer, refer to:

- the character being created
- the vocal skills used and the meaning created
- your response to the performance as an audience member. [15]

TIP

Check the notes you have made:

▶ Have you identified the performance or design focus of the question?

▶ Have you chosen the key moments or scenes you will write about?

▶ If appropriate, have you addressed each of the bullet points?

TIP

Some students make their plans on their question paper, making sure that they are including key words and any bullet point prompts.

TIP

Try to memorise a few lines from the play so that you can refer either to how they were delivered by the actors or what design choices occurred at that moment.

Making a plan

Once you have identified the focus of the question, take a minute or two to make a quick plan. This will help to ensure that you cover all necessary points and avoid repetition. There are many ways of making plans. Here are some possibilities.

Quick paragraph plan

This is a way of quickly deciding where you will cover the demands of the question. If, for example, you are asked to write about …

> an actor's use of physical and vocal skills in two scenes in relation to the style and genre of the production

… you might make a paragraph plan like this:

Paragraph 1

Name of play [*A Midsummer Night's Dream*].

Where and when I saw it.

Genre/style: period comedy.

Actor playing Helena.

Paragraph 2

Act 1, Scene 1: 'How happy some o'er other some can be!'

Vocal skills: Verse-speaking, emotional range, unhappy, emphasises negative words, sad, pleading tone.

Physical skills: Eye contact: stares after Hermia and Lysander when they leave, then looks at audience, gestures, points at herself. Change in posture at end. How she exits.

Effect/evaluation: Gains sympathy, speaks verse well, but could she have been more comic?

Paragraph 3

Act 2, Scene 2: 'Where was I to this keen mockery born?'

Vocal skills: Outraged tone, volume, reprimands, emphasis.

Physical skills: Pushes Lysander away, moves around stage to avoid him. Hunches her posture on 'insufficiency'. Tries to exit, but is held by Lysander. Stares wildly at him.

Effect/evaluation: Physical comedy is very funny and audience is aware of her dilemma, even if she doesn't understand it.

A bullet-point list

These are quick notes just to keep your answer on target. For example, using a set design example from *A Midsummer Night's Dream*:

Act 1, Scene 1: Theseus' Court

▶ Style: Period.

▶ Designer's skills: White columns, pale, neutral colour palette, smooth surfaces, large scale, symmetrical. Steps suggest power. Hippolyta, isolated behind barrier.

▶ Effect: Creates location (ancient Athens); sense of order and law.

▶ Evaluation: Impressive and beautiful, but perhaps bland? Over emphasis on imprisonment?

Act 2, Scene 2: Forest

▶ Style: Fantasy.

▶ Designer's skill: Explosion of colour: green hues, with bursts of purples and pinks. Onstage levels created by one tall and several 'fallen' trees, used by performers to stand on and trip over. Textured ground covering. Pool of water upstage.

▶ Effect: Contrasting wildness and chaos of forest, where magic can happen. Comic business on trees adds to comedy.

▶ Evaluation: Exciting to audience, especially use of pool and climbing the tree.

A mind map

This is a visual way of noting your ideas quickly. A plan for a question on the lighting design for *A Midsummer Night's Dream*, might look something like this:

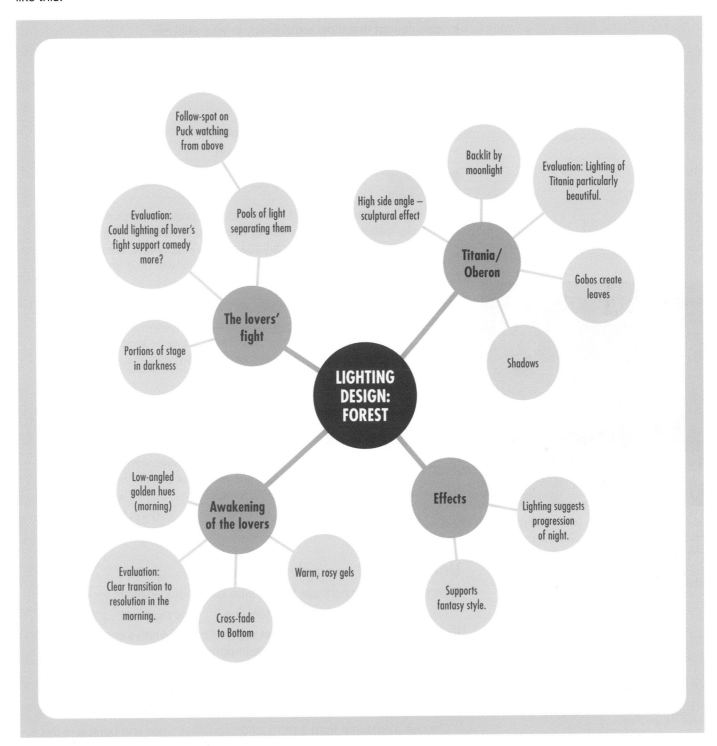

Choose one of the questions from page 65 and make a plan for it using the paragraph, bullet-list or mind-map method.

Demonstrating your understanding and skills

In the exam paper, you are being asked to demonstrate that you can:

▶ analyse an element of a production

▶ provide details from the production to support your analysis

▶ use correct theatrical terminology in your analysis

▶ evaluate the success of the specified aspect of the production.

In addition, you may need to show your understanding of:

▶ the period/setting of the production

▶ characters and their backgrounds

▶ the style and/or genre of the production

▶ the themes and aims of the production.

TASK 3

You need to make sure that the details you provide support your analysis, rather than simply listing what you have seen. Read the following extracts from two candidate-style responses. Then decide which is more successful at linking the details with their analysis.

> a Titania was dressed in a beautiful costume. It was a long, sleeveless, green gown in green silk. There were green and pink petals sewn onto the train of its skirt. She wore sandals that were tied to her ankles. She wore her hair down and she may have had a hairpiece, because it was very long.
>
> b In order to create a regal appearance for Titania, the costume designer dressed her in a long, green, silk **empire-line** dress with a dramatic train, that was carried by the fairies. The designer also made clear that this was no ordinary queen, as the dress was embroidered with gold thread and embellished with a colourful assortment of leaves, petals, and insects in a shiny, translucent fabric, which fluttered when she moved. The impact was both beautiful and startling, in keeping with the magical, fantasy world.

▲ *A modern design for Titania (Aaliyah Habeeb), using regal purples and greys. Her cape, headdress and shell jewellery, in particular, set her above the other characters in the forest.*

Using detailed examples

Words which examiners use to describe successful answers include:

> confident   balanced   thorough   fully explored   detailed.

Examiners reward examples which support the evaluative conclusions made by the students. It is therefore important that you keep in mind examples from the production which will support your opinion of it.

TASK 4

Choose a costume from a production you have seen and complete the following chart. An example has been given to guide you.

Details and examples	Analysis	Impact/evaluation
Character is barefoot and dressed in ragged, soiled clothing.	Condition suggests the character lives in poverty.	This was [or was not] effective because …

The concept or artistic intentions of a production

You may be asked to evaluate how aspects of a production aimed to fulfil a concept or artistic intentions. This means what the director and production team hoped to achieve and what creative choices were made to achieve it. You might, for example, have seen a play about the difficulties of those returning from a war. The concept or artistic intentions might have been to use all the production elements to help the audience experience the characters' pain. To make this vivid for the audience, performers and designers could use:

▶ staging/blocking, perhaps even having the characters walk through the audience, shouting at them

▶ sound, for example having speakers at the back and sides of auditorium so the audience is surrounded by sound

▶ lighting, such as strobe or other flashing lights, to show when a character is having a breakdown or experiencing a flashback

▶ military costumes for flashback scenes

▶ the set of a realistic British room, within the rubble of a foreign war.

All of these choices would reinforce the artistic intention of conveying that the war remains with the characters.

TASK 5

Ask yourself what you think the artistic intention was for the show you saw. Create a bullet-point list, like the one on the left, giving examples of how the different production elements contributed to that intention.

Improving the quality of your written expression

It is the quality of your ideas that is most important, but good writing habits will make your work clearer and more effective. Some advice is given below on how to improve your written expression.

▶ Ensure you can spell the title of the play and the main characters' names. This will help to avoid confusion.

▶ Organise your ideas so it is clear when you are writing about more than one character or scene:
The two characters I will contrast are …
The first key scene is …

▶ Use words and phrases to show that you are analysing:
The effect of this was …
This was done in order to …
This was accomplished by …

▶ Include evaluative vocabulary:
This successfully conveyed …
Unfortunately, the costume lacked the necessary impact …
This believably showed …

▶ Incorporate key words from the question to ensure that you are answering with the correct focus.

Was it repetitive?

Was the pace too slow?

Did it lack variety?

If writing a negative comment, avoid words like 'boring' or 'bad', as they may suggest that you have not tried to engage with the production. If you found something confusing or dull, try to analyse why.

Did the staging make it difficult to see or hear?

Offer something constructive to show that you are a knowledgeable theatre-goer.

Troubleshooting common problems

Common shortcomings in responses in this exam include:

- ▶ not answering the specific question
- ▶ lack of detail and terminology
- ▶ not covering a range of skills
- ▶ only describing, rather than analysing and evaluating
- ▶ not considering the impact on the audience and themselves
- ▶ not offering a personal response.

The following tips address these issues and should help you to improve your writing.

Answer the specific question

Every year, there are candidates who do not answer the question asked. They may instead answer a previous year's question that they had revised for, or another one for which they have prepared, or simply what they wish they had been asked. To avoid this, underline the key words in the question and keep checking that you have addressed them accurately.

Frequent symptoms of misreading of questions include:

- ▶ writing about a different section of the play or the wrong number of scenes, if specified (If you are asked to write about **two** scenes, then that is what you must do.)
- ▶ writing too generally about the subject (If asked specifically about vocal skills, don't instead write about all acting skills, such as movement.)
- ▶ forgetting to identify the style or genre of the play, if asked
- ▶ ignoring the bullet-point prompts, if provided.

TASK 6

The writer of the example below has been asked to analyse and evaluate the use of sound design in two scenes of the production. Read their response and identify how they could have improved their answer.

> At the climax of the play, the sound started very quietly, but then became very loud. The loudness was almost deafening to us in the audience. Then, it suddenly became quiet. This was very startling, changing as it did from soft to loud to silent. I believe the sound designer wanted to draw attention to this moment for some reason.

TIP

Midway through your response, double-check that you have included the key words from the question in your response. If not, fold them in as you finish.

Without regard to the demands of the question, some students will write all of their impressions of a production. While you may feel satisfied at the amount you have written, if it doesn't answer the question, you will not be rewarded. You should aim to prepare for a variety of questions, but don't expect to get exactly the question you want.

Include detail and terminology

Make sure that you have prepared this knowledge well in advance of the exam. Use the grids, charts, examples and glossary in this book to nail these areas. Prepare several key moments, performances, costumes, and so on which you feel confident writing about.

It isn't advisable to write in an overly prescriptive way, but the following examples could help you to structure your sentences and paragraphs.

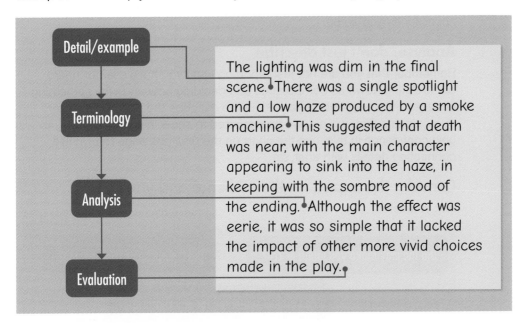

Detail/example → Terminology → Analysis → Evaluation

The lighting was dim in the final scene. There was a single spotlight and a low haze produced by a smoke machine. This suggested that death was near, with the main character appearing to sink into the haze, in keeping with the sombre mood of the ending. Although the effect was eerie, it was so simple that it lacked the impact of other more vivid choices made in the play.

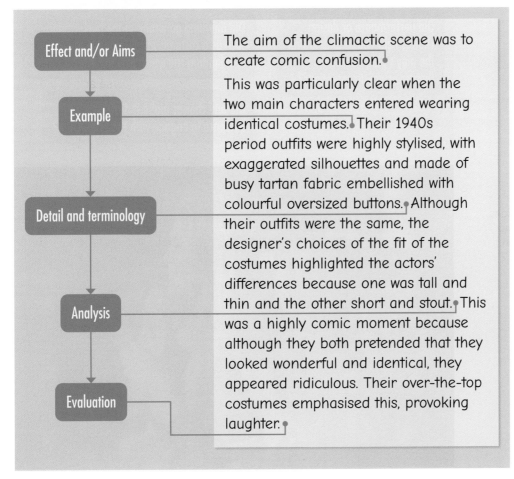

Effect and/or Aims → Example → Detail and terminology → Analysis → Evaluation

The aim of the climactic scene was to create comic confusion.

This was particularly clear when the two main characters entered wearing identical costumes. Their 1940s period outfits were highly stylised, with exaggerated silhouettes and made of busy tartan fabric embellished with colourful oversized buttons. Although their outfits were the same, the designer's choices of the fit of the costumes highlighted the actors' differences because one was tall and thin and the other short and stout. This was a highly comic moment because although they both pretended that they looked wonderful and identical, they appeared ridiculous. Their over-the-top costumes emphasised this, provoking laughter.

TIP

You will not get more points for repeating the same point. You need to make a range of points.

TIP

Evaluation points may be positive or negative or a combination of them.

TIP

Some exam boards provide suggestions in the exam paper about how long you should spend on a particular question.

Cover a range of skills

If you are asked to write about physical skills and you focus only on gestures, or if you only refer to colours when asked about costume design, you cannot get a high mark. You need to show that you understand the variety of skills a performer or designer might employ. For physical acting skills, for example, you could write about movement, stance, posture, **gait**, facial expressions, proximity and use of stage space. For costume design, you might write about colours, textures, fit, condition, fabric, silhouette, accessories and so on.

Analyse, don't just describe

Remember that you are not just reporting what you have seen or heard, but breaking down its components and deciding how and why something occurred. You will never be asked just to describe the plot, a character or a costume. You will always be expected to show insight into them. To gain confidence in this, use the chart on the previous page to practise connecting details with analysis.

Consider the impact on the audience and yourself

Ask yourself:

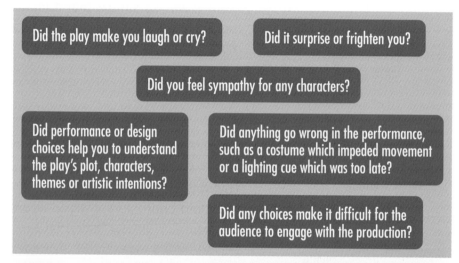

Did the play make you laugh or cry?

Did it surprise or frighten you?

Did you feel sympathy for any characters?

Did performance or design choices help you to understand the play's plot, characters, themes or artistic intentions?

Did anything go wrong in the performance, such as a costume which impeded movement or a lighting cue which was too late?

Did any choices make it difficult for the audience to engage with the production?

Offer a personal response

In addition to your understanding of the impact of theatre makers' choices on the audience, most exam boards welcome your personal response. Some specifically ask for it. Below are some words and phrases to help you express your response.

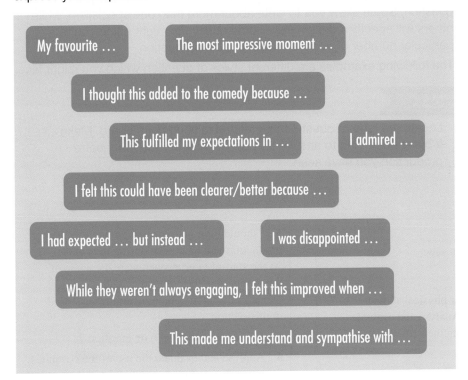

My favourite …

The most impressive moment …

I thought this added to the comedy because …

This fulfilled my expectations in …

I admired …

I felt this could have been clearer/better because …

I had expected … but instead …

I was disappointed …

While they weren't always engaging, I felt this improved when …

This made me understand and sympathise with …

Timing

This is not an exam where you should expect to have time left over at the end. Every minute needs to be used wisely. As the Live Theatre question is usually the last one in the paper, it may be the one that is most rushed. To avoid this:

▶ note how much time you have for the whole paper

▶ consider how to divide that across the questions

▶ spend more time on the questions worth the most marks

▶ use a quick plan to avoid repetition or running out of ideas

▶ avoid a lengthy introduction (or conclusion) where you might repeat yourself: begin earning marks right away

▶ beforehand, practise writing under timed conditions.

 TIP

Don't spend too long on questions worth only a few marks. If a question is only worth, say, four marks, you will never be awarded more than that, no matter how long your answer is.

EXAM-STYLE PRACTICE QUESTIONS

 TIP

If you want more practice questions, adapt the questions from the other exam boards to the style of your board and then answer or make plans for those.

Each exam board will ask you to analyse and evaluate an aspect of the production you have seen. Some will offer a choice of questions; some expect you to answer more than one question; and some ask you only one question. Some allow you to write about more than one specialism, while others will specify a design skill. Some questions might guide you to a particular number of scenes or section of a production.

The following examples are different styles of question which you might face.

TASK

Locate the type of question that relates to your exam board. Make a bullet point plan to answer that question about the live theatre production you have seen.

AQA

Answer **one** question from this section.

State the title of the live theatre production you saw:

EITHER

1 Describe how one or more actors used their physical skills to interpret their role within the production. Analyse and evaluate how successful they were in communicating their role to the audience.
You could make reference to:
- movement and use of stage space
- gestures
- posture and gait
- a scene or section and/or the production as a whole. [32]

OR

2 Describe how the set was used to communicate mood and action in the production. Analyse and evaluate how successful the set design was in helping to communicate meaning to the audience.
You could make reference to
- type of set and materials used
- size, shape, colours and furnishings
- a scene or section and/or the production as a whole. [32]

OR

3 Describe how sound was used to support the style and context of the production. Analyse and evaluate how successful the sound design was in communicating the meaning and style of the production to the audience.
You could make reference to:
- sound effects
- music
- how sound was created and amplified
- a scene or section and/or the production as a whole. [32]

WJEC

You should base your answer on one live theatre production you have seen during the course.
At the start of your answer, state the name of the production, the company and the venue.
Quality of written communication is assessed in this section.

Answer **either** question 6 **or** question 7.

6 Analyse and evaluate the use of the costumes in two key scenes to communicate the director's interpretation of the play to the audience. In your answer, refer to:
- the style of the production
- how the costumes are used to communicate the director's interpretation and support the actors' characterisations in the production
- your response to the performance as an audience member. [15]

OR

7 Analyse and evaluate the use of vocal skills in two key scenes to communicate the characters and the action of the play to the audience. In your answer, refer to:
- the style of the production
- the vocal skills used and how they create character and support the meaning of the play
- your response to the performance as an audience member. [15]

Edexcel

Answer **both** questions on the performance you have seen.

Write the title, venue and date of the performance you have seen in the space below:

a   Analyse how one or more actors use their physical skills to engage the audience
   at the end of the play.   [6]

b   Evaluate how the lighting design created impact within
   the performance.   [9]

OCR

You must answer this question referring to a different performance text from the one you
have studied for Section A.

At the start of your answer, write the name, venue and date (month and year) of the live
performance you have seen. Include examples from this performance in your answer.

Evaluate how successfully the style and meaning of the play was communicated to you by
the acting skills in the live performance you have seen.

In your answer, you should consider:

• what you felt the style and meaning were
• how effectively one or more performers created meaning
• what skills the performers used and their impact on you.

You should use appropriate drama and theatre terminology.   [30]

Eduqas

Answer **either** question 6 **or** 7.

You should base your answer on one live theatre production seen during the course. You
must use a different text from the one you use in Section A.

At the start of your answer, you should state the name of the production, the company and
the venue.

EITHER

6   Analyse and evaluate how the set and lighting are used in two key scenes to create
   interest and communicate meaning to the audience.
   In your answer, refer to:
   • the style of the production
   • how the set and lighting are used to create mood and to communicate meaning
   • your response to the performance as an audience member.   [15]

OR

7   Analyse and evaluate how acting skills are used by an actor in two key scenes to create
   character and meaning for the audience.
   In your answer, refer to:
   • the style of the production
   • how acting skills are used to create character and further the action of the play
   • your response to the performance as an audience member.   [15]

GLOSSARY

Acoustics: The sound quality of a given space, including how the size and shape of the theatre affects the warmth or clarity of sound.

Actor-musicians: Performers who play musical instruments as part of their acting roles.

Aesthetic: An approach to design or art with clear ideas as to what is correct or beautiful.

Ambience: The quality, character, feeling or nature of a place, such as a bustling city or an isolated farm.

Amphitheatre: A circular stage, with the audience in curved seating on a steep slope around the front portion of the circle. Amphitheatres are often outdoor theatres, like those of ancient Greece, but some large indoor spaces have been based on their design.

Anachronistic: Inappropriate for a time period being portrayed, for example from a much earlier or, more commonly, later period, such as a laptop in the 17th century.

Aperture: An opening, hole or gap.

Apron: An area at the front of proscenium stages which is still visible to the audience when the curtains are closed.

Artistic intention: The choices made by theatre makers about what they want to communicate to an audience and how they will do it.

Audience interaction: Involving the audience in the play, for example by giving them props, using **direct address** or bringing them on stage.

Aural: What is heard.

Backdrop: A large painted cloth hung, usually at the back of the stage, as part of the scenery.

Backlighting: Lighting projected from a source upstage. It highlights the outline of actors or scenery and separates them from the background.

Blackout: When all stage lights are turned off. This can be sudden or gradual.

Blocking: The actors' movements. These are usually set during rehearsals in collaboration with the director.

Box set: A setting of a complete room, often naturalistic, with three walls and a 'missing' fourth wall facing the audience.

Candelabra: A large candlestick with curved arms that can hold several candles.

Characterisation: How an actor creates a role through their understanding of the character's background, motivations and importance in the play.

Climax: The most intense section of the play, often when the narrative reaches its most important point.

Colour-coding: Using certain colours to convey specific meanings, such as social class or membership of a group.

Colour palette: The range of colours used, such as muted tones, autumn tones, primary colours, black and white; complementary or clashing.

Composer: Someone who writes music. Some productions have a composer to create original music.

Concept: A unifying idea about the production, such as how it will be interpreted or performed.

Configuration: The type of stage and audience arrangement, for example end on, thrust, in the round and so on.

Contemporary: Of the present day, modern.

Context: The circumstances of the setting of a play, such as the location, period of time or conventions. These might be historical, geographical and cultural.

Contrapuntal: Working as a counterpoint or contrast to, such as sad music with a happy image.

Conventions: Theatrical techniques used in and associated with particular types of performance, such as speaking directly to the audience or miming the use of props.

Couture: Expensive, specially made fashionable designer clothing.

Crescendo: Increasing in loudness or the loudest point, often of music.

Cross-fade: When one area of lighting slowly dims while another area fades up.

Cue timing: The time it takes for a lighting change, for example the counts until a blackout occurs or how long a cross-fade takes.

Curtain call: When the actors take their bows at the end of the performance.

Curtain-call music: Music played during the curtain call. Sometimes the curtain call is choreographed to a song.

Cyclorama: A large semi-circular stretched curtain or screen, usually positioned upstage. This is often used to depict a background, such as the sky.

Diagonals: Lights projected down at roughly a 45-degree angle.

Direct address: When a character speaks directly to the audience.

Discordant: Unpleasant, inharmonious, harsh or clashing.

Documentary: Pictures, films, recordings or other materials from interviews or reports of real events.

Double-take: A comic technique, when a character looks at something twice, because they didn't believe or grasp what they saw the first time.

Douse: Extinguish a light.

Downlight or **top-light:** Light from directly overhead.

Drapes: Curtains or other hanging fabric.

Empire line: The shape of a high-waisted dress, often with a low neckline.

End on: A staging configuration in which the audience sits along one end of the stage directly facing it.

Episodic: A structure involving a series of scenes, or 'episodes', which are often short and might take place in several locations.

Expressionistic: Non-realistic; based more on emotions, impressions and themes.

Fade: Gradually turn sound or lights up or down.

Fantasy: Something which cannot occur in the real world, or a design which creates an unrealistic world, such as fairy tales, myths, the supernatural and science fiction.

Farce: A broad type of comedy which often employs stereotypical characters, unlikely coincidences and extreme situations.

Filter or **gel:** A coloured piece of plastic inserted into a case on a lantern to alter the colour of the light.

Flat: A piece of scenery, often painted, mounted on a tall frame.

Flies: The space above the stage, usually out of view of the audience, used to store items or lower ('fly') items onto the stage.

Floor coverings: Any covering of the stage floor, such as a wooden effect to appear like floorboards, or linoleum for a kitchen floor.

Floor lighting: Lanterns placed on low stands, often used to cast shadows.

Fly system: A means of raising and lowering scenery or other items onto the stage using a system of ropes and pulleys. To raise or lower scenery from this area is to 'fly a set in'.

Follow-spot: A lamp that produces a bright beam, which can be used to 'follow' a performance.

Footlights: Low lights placed on the downstage edge. Popular in Victorian theatres and sometimes now used to create period lighting effects.

Fourth wall: An imaginary barrier between the audience and the stage. A performer might 'break the fourth wall' and speak directly to, or otherwise interact with, the audience.

Furnishings: Furniture on the set, such as chairs, cushions and tables.

Gait: How a character walks, such as stiffly, or limps, stomps, shuffles and so on.

Gauze: Curtains that might hang loose or be mounted on a frame, which, if lit a certain way, are transparent.

Gel: *See* **Filter**.

Genre: A category or type of drama such as comedy, tragedy or musical theatre, usually with its own conventions.

Gesture: A movement of a part of a body, often hand, arms or head, such as waving, nodding or reaching out.

Gobo: A metal, glass or plastic cut-out attached to a lantern to project patterns, such as leaves, stars, swirls or waves.

Hosiery: Tights, stockings or socks; plain or patterned; skin-tone or coloured.

House lights: The lights in the auditorium that are usually o while the audience is being seated and then dimmed when the performance is about to begin.

Hybrid: A mixture of two or more things or types.

Immersive: A production in which the audience is made to feel part of the world of the play.

Intensity: How bright, powerful or forceful something is.

Intonation: The rise and fall of pitch in the voice; the musicality of speech.

Jacobean revenge tragedy: A dramatic genre of plays popular in the late 16th and early 17th centuries. The plays involve a character seeking revenge on others with violent results.

Lantern: A lamp and reflector in a box which produces lighting. There are different types of lantern, such as profile, fresnel and flood.

LED lights: Powerful and colourful lights that don't require gels and are energy efficient.

GLOSSARY

Lighting plot: Like an architectural plan to show where the lights will hang. It will indicate the position, type of lighting fixture and colours of gels.

Lighting rig: The structure that holds the lighting equipment in the theatre.

Live sound: Sound created by the stage management, technicians or actors during the performance.

Melodrama: A highly dramatic piece designed to provoke emotions in the audience, usually associated with stereotypical characters and extreme situations.

Microphone: A device for converting and amplifying sound.

Mimicry: Imitation; copying someone's speech and mannerisms, possibly in a mocking way.

Modern dress: Costumes from the time in which the play is being performed rather than when it is set, for example 21st-century costumes in a play originally set in the 17th century.

Montage: A collection or composite of different images, words or music.

Motif: A recurring design; in music, it is a short musical phrase which might be repeated.

Motivated sound: Sound required by a script, such as telephone ringing or a doorbell.

Motivation: What compels a character to do something, such as their desires or needs.

Moving light: Either a lighting fixture manually moved by an operator or a computer-operated fixture which is moved remotely.

Multimedia: Consisting of a variety of media formats, such as photographs, slides, animation, audio and film.

Multi-roling: One actor playing more than one character.

Musical instruments: Drums, guitars, violins and so on, which might be played by a band, orchestra or actors.

Music hall: Popular variety entertainment, associated with theatres of the Victorian age and the early 20th century.

Naturalistic: Lifelike, believable, realistic, based in the 'real' world.

Non-linear: Not in actual event order; non-chronological.

Overheads: Microphones hung above the stage to boost the overall sound.

Parchment: An old material for writing on; a stiff thin light-brown/ beige or off-white paper.

Period: The era or date in which something is set. A 'period production' refers to a production set at an earlier time.

Physical comedy: Comic skills, such as mime, pratfalls and physical stunts.

Platform: A raised area on the stage.

Promenade: A type of theatre where the audience are required to move around to follow the actors.

Posture: How a character stands, such as upright, hunched or slumped.

Practical lights: Working onstage lights that are used in the set, such as desk lamps, torches or candles.

Pratfall: A silly or embarrassing fall, often used in physical comedies.

Pre-show music: Music played as the audience enters and waits for the performance to begin.

Projection: A film or still image projected to form a theatrical backdrop.

Props: Moveable items on the stage, including hand props that the actors can carry, including books, cups and phones.

Proximity: The distance between characters or things; how near or far apart they are.

Pyrotechnics: Special effects that create dramatic features, such as fireworks, explosions or flashes.

Radio mics: Portable microphones, often worn, which allow actors and singers to be amplified with no visible means of connection.

Ramp: A sloped pathway which may be used for walking on or for wheeled transportation.

Recorded sound: Sound that has been recorded specially for playback during the performance or selected from sound effects archives.

Restoration comedy: A stylised comedy from the 17th century, which focused on society manners and intrigues.

Reveal: When something is unexpectedly shown to an audience. A reveal may be a plot twist or it could be a design feature.

Reverb: An echoing effect, sustaining the sound longer than usual.

Revolve: A large turntable device that can be turned to reveal a different setting.

Scaffolding: A large structure, usually of boards and metal poles, which creates different levels on a set.

Sconce: A candle-holder that can be attached to a wall.

Scrims: *See* **Gauze***.*

Set dressings: Items on the set not used as props, but which create detail and interest, such as vases or framed paintings.

Sightline: The audience's view of the stage/performance.

Smoke, fog or haze machine: A piece of equipment which uses a gas to produce clouds or mists.

Snap: Turn sound suddenly off or on.

Sound effects: Special sounds created either live or recorded, such as slamming doors or alarm bells.

Speaker: A device for amplifying and projecting sound. The placement of speakers will influence how the audience experiences the sound.

Special effects: Unusual sounds, mechanical devices or visuals, such as explosions, trapdoors or storm sequences.

Spectacle: Something with visual impact; an event which is exciting to watch.

Spotlight: A lamp that projects a bright light onto an area of stage, usually focusing on a performer.

Stairs: Steps from one level of the set to another. In some productions, grand staircases are a design feature.

Stance: How a character stands, such as feet wide apart or turned in.

Stereotypical: Qualities commonly believed, but not necessarily true; overly-simplified, such as a stereotypical villain.

Storytelling: A type of non-realistic theatre which often focuses on techniques like narration, simple scenery and multi-roling to convey a story, often a fable or fairy tale, to an audience.

Strip light: A long, thin glass tube of light, often with a plastic cover.

Strobe: A lighting device that gives short, bright bursts of bright light.

Style: The identifiable features of the way in which something is created or performed.

Stylised: Non-realistic, heightened, exaggerated; done in a manner that perhaps emphasises one element.

Sweetheart neckline: The neck of a garment shaped like the top of a heart: low in the centre front and rounded on either side.

Symbolic: Using something to represent something else, such as a rose to symbolise love.

Synchronised: Done at the same time, in unison, such as synchronised movement or speaking.

Synopsis: A brief summary of a story's plot or key events.

Tableau: A still image of a scene. It might focus on the pictorial aspect of the grouping, including the relationship of the different figures and how they are costumed.

Top-light: *See* **Downlight***.*

Train: A long section at the back of a garment which trails on the ground behind the wearer.

Transition: The change from one scene, location or mood to another.

Trapdoor: A door in the floor or ceiling of a stage allowing objects or performers to be dropped, lifted or lowered.

Trim: Additional decoration on a costume, typically on the edges and in a contrasting fabric or colour.

Truck: A platform on wheels upon which scenery can be mounted and moved.

Visual: What is seen.

Volume: How loud or soft a sound or voice is.

Wash: Light which covers the whole stage or large area of it.

Wind machine: Motorised theatrical equipment, usually positioned off stage, used to create the physical or aural effect of gusts of wind on stage.

Wings / Wing space: An area to the side of the stage from which actors can enter and from which props, furnishings or scenery can be moved onto the stage.

IMAGE ACKNOWLEDGEMENTS

p4 frantic00 from Shutterstock

p5 Chinnapong from Shutterstock

p8 Willy Barton / Shutterstock.com

p9 Donald Cooper / Photostage

p12 Geraint Lewis / Alamy Stock Photo

p13 Donald Cooper / Photostage

p14 emc design ltd

p19 Catherine Ashmore

p20 (top) Donald Cooper / Photostage; (bottom) Geraint Lewis / Alamy Stock Photo

p22 Marc Brenner

p24 Donald Cooper / Photostage

p25 (top) Brinkhoff/Mögenburg; (bottom) Paul Fox

p26 emc design ltd

p30 (top) Stephen Chung / Alamy Live News; (bottom) Rosie Elnile / Gate Theatre

p32 Helen Murray

p34 Paul Fox

p35 (top) Donald Cooper / Photostage; (bottom) Paul Fox

p36 emc design ltd

p38 emc design ltd

p40 (top) Joan Marcus / TCD/Prod.DB / Alamy Stock Photo; (bottom) Marc Brenner

p42 Marc Brenner / ArenaPAL

p44 Ali Müftüogullari on Unsplash

p45 (top left) Matt Crockett; (top right and bottom left) Paul Fox; (bottom right) Mark Douet

p46 emc design ltd

p50 Johan Persson

p52 Donald Cooper / Photostage

p54 Christopher Sinnott from Pixabay

p55 Anastasia Gepp from Pixabay, Tania Van den Berghen from Pixabay, ravindrameena556 from Pixabay, Fahri ramdani on Unsplash, Julia M Cameron from Pexels, Terricks Noah on Unsplash

p56 emc design ltd

p60 (top) a katz / Shutterstock.com; (bottom) Donald Cooper / Photostage

p62 Manuel Harlan

p63 Antonia Jater

p68 Alec Perkins at Creative Commons

p69 Lakeview Images at Shutterstock

p70 Kamira / Shutterstock.com

p72 Christian Bertrand / Shutterstock.com

p73 panitanphoto at Shutterstock.